20 Greatest Artists

Kalyani Mookherji is an alumnus of Jadavpur University, Kolkata, from where she finished her postgraduation in English Literature. She has been a writer and educator for over ten years now. She also runs a popular literary workshop for children, Feeling Bookerish, in Wellington, a town in The Nilgiris district of Tamil Nadu, where she currently resides after having travelled the length and breadth of India as an army wife.

Despite being a busy mom to a bright teen and a spoilt dog, Kalyani finds time for other interests such as music, baking, and blogging at crumbsonmynotebook.wordpress.com. Her other books include *100 Greatest Sportspersons* and *20 Greatest Philosophers*.

20 Greatest artists

KALYANI MOOKHERJI

Published by
Rupa Publications India Pvt. Ltd 2019
7/16, Ansari Road, Daryaganj
New Delhi 110002

Sales centres:
Allahabad Bengaluru Chennai
Hyderabad Jaipur Kathmandu
Kolkata Mumbai

Copyright © Kalyani Mookherji 2019

The views and opinions expressed in this book are the author's own and the facts are as reported by her which have been verified to the extent possible, and the publishers are not in any way liable for the same.

All rights reserved.

No part of this publication may be reproduced, transmitted, or stored in a retrieval system, in any form or by any means, electronic, mechanical, photocopying, recording or otherwise, without the prior permission of the publisher.

ISBN: 978-93-5333-426-0

First impression 2019

10 9 8 7 6 5 4 3 2 1

The moral right of the author has been asserted.

Printed by HT Media Ltd, Gr. Noida

This book is sold subject to the condition that it shall not, by way of trade or otherwise, be lent, resold, hired out, or otherwise circulated, without the publisher's prior consent, in any form of binding or cover other than that in which it is published.

*For Kalpita,
my 'Imagined One'*

Contents

Introduction	ix
1. Leonardo da Vinci	1
2. Michelangelo di Lodovico Buonarroti Simoni	9
3. Rembrandt Harmenszoon van Rijn	16
4. Johannes Vermeer	23
5. Peter Paul Rubens	31
6. Katsushika Hokusai	38
7. Claude Monet	44
8. Paul Cézanne	50
9. Abanindranath Tagore	58
10. Vincent Van Gogh	67
11. Georges Seurat	76
12. Frida Kahlo	82
13. Amrita Sher-Gil	89
14. Pablo Picasso	97

15. Georgia O'Keeffe	107
16. Edvard Munch	114
17. Salvador Dalí	121
18. Andy Warhol	128
19. Wu Guanzhong	136
20. Maqbool Fida Husain	144
Conclusion	155
Acknowledgements	157

Introduction

In his highly influential work, *The Mirror and the Lamp* (1953), American literary theorist M.H. Abrams introduced two metaphors within which all art may be understood. At one end is the 'Mirror' or art, which tries to depict the world as it exactly appears. This position is the foundation for Representative Art, which involves a realistic style and techniques such as perspective, effects of light and shade known as chiaroscuro, and so on.

At the other end is the 'Lamp' whose streaming light can be thought of as the artist's imagination, leading to his or her personal vision of art. This is the basis of Expressionist Art, an art form that is an expression of the artist's imagination, emotions and vision.

Of course, artistic styles cannot be straitjacketed into either of the above. Instead, all art that delights and moves us falls within a spectrum of styles. At one end of this spectrum is the purely imitative art which aims at mere photographic reproduction of the actual world. On the other end would be purely abstract art which only expresses the artist's own emotions and imagination.

Within the two ends of this spectrum, the best artists in history have been trying to portray newer ways of looking at the world. They have moved beyond copy-imitation to re-presenting the world according to their own vision of what is significant and worth highlighting to the viewers. Others have aspired for a more idealistic vision of reality—where the shoddiness of common scenes and human tendencies is not ignored but transcended, into the best that might be possible. This is especially true of the best religious paintings. Then again, there are artists who reject the representational style and try to see the world as an expression of their own states of mind and their concerns. But even this is not divorced from reality but rather based on the artist's own understanding of history, politics, relationships and other such dynamics.

Now, a little about the history of art till the Renaissance, where you meet the first of the artists of this book. The earliest known evidence of prehistoric art goes as far back as 290,000 BCE—that is more than two lakh years ago! And you will be proud to know that the location of this highly precious evidence is right here, in central India—at a cave complex in Bhimbetka in Madhya Pradesh. This art at Bhimbetka consists of petroglyphs (scratchings and engravings on the rock surface) and cupules or non-utilitarian cup-shaped depressions in the rock surface. Interestingly, the Bhimbetka cave complex reveals art that can be dated from the Lower Palaeolithic Age, through Mesolithic, Chalcolithic to the early historic period—in effect documenting the entire arc of human evolution.

Other examples of the earliest cave drawings have come from the famous Chauvet, Lascaux caves in France and Altamira in Spain dating back to as far as 50,000 BCE. These are mainly in the form of murals on cave walls chiefly depicting animals and hunting scenes but also some symbols and patterns showing that humans had started thinking in abstract forms. Chinese calligraphy is the other significant form of fine arts in the Neolithic Age.

The Bronze Age roughly covers 3500 BCE to 1500 BCE and includes art from the ancient Persian, Sumerian, Babylonian and Egyptian civilizations. The ancient Egyptians were the first to create what we would recognize as paintings today—depicting the human subject partly in profile and partly from the front. They were also the first to develop painting conventions on how gods, humans and other creatures were to be depicted. The illustrated manuscripts of Persia and the frescoes and vase paintings of ancient Minoan civilization are other instances of fine arts from the Bronze Age.

In the Iron Age, the Mycenaean civilization of Ancient Greece came up with more refined artistic expressions in their tempera frescoes, sculpture, pottery, precious jewellery and metalwork. The heights of cultural expression were, however, achieved by ancient Greek art from 1100 BCE to 100 BCE. This was the time of renowned Greek painters like Zeuxis, Apelles and Parrhasius, whose artistic innovations included techniques of highlighting, shading and colouring. Panel-paintings became highly valued and were made in tempera or encaustic paint.

Later, ancient Roman art carried on the conventions of their Greek predecessors, though the tone moved from the realistic to the heroic with painters primarily interested in depicting the military exploits of Roman heroes.

Western Art in the Medieval Age was primarily characterized by the dominance of Christian themes and figures like the Virgin, Baby Jesus, the adult Christ as well as innumerable saints and martyrs. Byzantine painting from this time has many exquisite examples of panel-painting and miniature-painting as well as manuscript illumination. Irish Christian Art from this time includes their decorated and illuminated Gospel manuscripts. In India on the other hand, the murals in the Ajanta caves and the large frescoes in the Ellora caves are examples of the influence of Buddhist art. Soon, the artists under Hindu kings copied this as evident from the frescoes decorating the Chola temple of Brihadisvara at Thanjavur in Tamil Nadu as well as the murals on temple walls in Pundareekapuram, Ettumanoor, Aymanam and

INTRODUCTION

Thiruvananthapuram in Kerala.

With the arrival of the fourteenth century in Europe, a breath of fresh air began blowing through the Western world of arts, culture, education and learning. Firstly, artists and intellectuals replaced the Christian view of the world with a humanistic worldview, which shifted the gaze on to Man—literally, in the field of visual arts. Secondly, there was a new appreciation of the themes, conventions and styles of art and culture from Classical Antiquity, which further encouraged a secular worldview.

The Renaissance thus brought about a new way of seeing the world and it is at this point that you get to meet the first artist of this book—Leonardo da Vinci. He is followed by the other great Renaissance painter and sculptor, Michelangelo. Rembrandt, Vermeer and Rubens were the other artists marking significant developments in representation of the world, often marrying newly emerging scientific knowledge to artistic techniques. But, by the end of nineteenth century, there was a growing weariness with the convention of depicting the world with detailed realism. Instead, artists wished to portray the scenes around them as they appeared at that moment, as an effect of the light, wind and other elements. This led to a new style of painting known as Impressionism which influenced greats like Monet, Van Gogh, Cézanne and Seurat.

Soon, though, with new interest in the human mind

and psychology, the inner world of the artist's dreams, fantasies and symbols began to take precedence. Art became increasingly a personal vision of the world or an expression of the artist's own state of mind, as seen in the works of Picasso, Dalí and Munch. This wave of innovation in European art could not but affect artists in other parts of the world. And yet, for artists in India, China, Japan and Mexico, it was not enough to copy European techniques and styles. The depiction of their own people, land and sky demanded an adaptation of traditional techniques and themes as evident in the art of Tagore, Hokusai, Guanzhong and Husain. Indeed, in the case of Tagore and later Guanzhong, their art would also figure as a significant aspect on the discourse of nationalism and culture. Similarly, women artists like Kahlo, O'Keeffe and Sher-Gil would find art a crucial way of negotiating issues like femininity, sexuality and identity in a world dominated by male artists and symbols.

Towards the middle of the twentieth century, the very meaning of art began to change. With themes like common objects of daily life and quicker techniques of mass production like print-making, artists like Andy Warhol threw open the exclusivity and complexity hitherto associated with fine arts. The world and its myriad subjects now could only be expressed by breaking all conventions of media, genre and techniques that had guided artists of previous centuries. Artists were ready to engage with

INTRODUCTION

themes of consumerism and popular culture as well as techniques of mass production and consumption. The aim was, above all, to make viewers stop in their tracks and reflect—on life and...well, art!

1. Leonardo da Vinci

The effect of light and shade is so real that the subject seems to live and breathe on the canvas. The lines direct the eye straight to the subject. And the luminosity of the expression on the face of the subject leaves the viewer mesmerized. It is not for nothing then, that Leonardo da Vinci is famous as one of the greatest artists in the history of humankind. He was the first to capture the play of light, shade, colour, line and tone and depict them on canvas. Techniques like perspective, chiaroscuro and sfumato (a blending of outline and colours to give a smoky appearance to the background) were popularized, if not developed, by him. Most remarkable of all—like a true Renaissance Man, da Vinci's skills far exceeded the canvas. Besides being a painter, he was a sculptor, inventor, architect, engineer, musician, writer and mathematician, while his interests extended to anatomy, geology, astronomy, botany and the emerging science of cartography.

Early Life

Born in 1452 as the illegitimate son of Messer Piero, a notary, and Caterina, a peasant woman, Leonardo spent the earliest part of his childhood with his mother in the region of Vinci, which comprised the valley of the Arno River near Florence. He spent the later part of his childhood with his father's family, where he received a basic school education. More importantly, this was the time when he first started keeping journals that would later prove invaluable in his artistic and creative endeavours.

In 1466, Leonardo was sent to Florence as an apprentice to an established artist, Andrea del Verrocchio, under whom he received a thorough grounding in anatomy, botany, optics, geology, geometry and perspective—all of which were customary for an aspiring artist. In those days, arts and sciences were not taught as separate subjects as they are now. An artist's apprentice was expected to be educated in scientific and mathematical concepts. Thus, da Vinci acquired a wide range of technical skills such as drafting, set construction, plaster-making, paint chemistry and metallurgy at the workshop. By the age of twenty, he had risen to the position of Master Craftsman of the guild, and even had his own studio—something unimaginable for someone so young.

Growing Fame

From Florence, da Vinci next moved to Milan where he sought the patronage of Duke Ludovico Sforza in return for various kinds of military inventions. For the next seventeen years, da Vinci continued to paint, sculpt, design and invent a whole lot of projects which made this period the most productive in his life. Among his earliest masterpieces was Virgin of the Rocks, depicting traits for which da Vinci would become famous later. The lush vegetation in the background gives depth of perspective to his painting while the pyramidal arrangement marks it as one belonging to the High Renaissance art tradition. This painting also provides evidence of the earliest use of sfumato, which he would use to perfection in Mona Lisa. Yet another Renaissance painting characteristic that da Vinci would use with consummate skill was the depiction of movement and expression. Thus, though the subjects were religious—the Virgin, Child Jesus and myriad other saints and apostles—their appearance and actions were humanized and animated with exquisite details. All these stylistic elements distinguish da Vinci's paintings from his early to mid-career, like Lady with an Ermine, Bacchus, The Annunciation and the Madonna series.

Among his drawings, the work that is most readily recognized today is The Vitruvian Man. The 1485 masterpiece shows two positions of a man superimposed on each other. In one position, his legs are close together and arms outstretched, thus marking the volume of a square. In the second position, the man's legs are placed apart while his arms are slightly raised, extended to indicate the circumference of a circle. In this drawing, da Vinci gives evidence of his studies in anatomy and geometry. At the same time, the drawing is not a bland scientific diagram—the delicate drawing of hair and its shading lent it a three-dimensional graphic look. This drawing has gone down in history as the ideal Renaissance figure and an icon of Humanist positivism. The anthropocentric optimism of the drawing revelled in the thought of the endless possibilities facing the human species at the time.

The other major artwork from the early half of his artistic career was The Last Supper, completed in 1498. This was commissioned by the Duke of Milan, Ludovico Sforza, for the refectory of the Convent of Santa Maria delle Grazie. Never before had a painting of such scale depicted such dramatic intensity, nor executed with such technical brilliance. Additionally, this was one of the earliest examples of da Vinci's vanishing point technique. This technique allowed the painting to blend into the surrounding spaces, giving an impression of natural extension of the room—a technique which would greatly influence mural paintings and would be adopted by da Vinci's own contemporaries, such as Michelangelo and Raphael.

Later Phase

The invasion of Milan by the French forced da Vinci to leave Florence, and he spent the remaining years of his life travelling to cities like Venice and Rome to work on different projects. The endeavours of this part of his life reveal a more refined technique, evident not only in paintings such as Salvator Mundi (1500) and Mona Lisa (1503) but in drawings too, such as The Virgin and Child with St. Anne and St. John the Baptist (circa 1499-1500). This was probably created as a 'pre-drawing' to serve as a guide for a painting according to artistic conventions of those times. Even then, the huge drawing boasts of an amazing level of detailing, besides a high level of naturalism in its chalk and charcoal lines.

Salvator Mundi was commissioned by King Louis XVII of France after his conquest of Milan in 1499. The painting depicts Jesus in the role of the saviour of the world marked by right hand raised in benediction as well as the master of the universe exemplified by the crystalline sphere in the other. What is remarkable about the painting is the way Jesus has been humanized — dressed in Renaissance robes of the time as well as bearing a soft gaze, acquired through da Vinci's growing expertise in the sfumato technique. And yet, the appearance of light emanating from the chest, as it were, as well as the glowing fingers, imbue the figure with a deeply spiritual quality.

It is as the creator of Mona Lisa however that the world knows da Vinci most widely. This 1503 painting is a portrait of Lisa Gherardini, the wife of a Florentine merchant named Francesco del Gioconda, also known by the title La Gioconda. The portrait shows all the signature techniques of da Vinci such as the sfumato, imbuing the subject with a pleasing calmness, as well as the chiaroscuro technique, lending a profound depth to the painting. However, it was da Vinci's intense realism that set him apart from the artists of the time. In early Renaissance portraits, though the subject would be depicted through minute technical detailing, the personality was left to be interpreted through symbols like objects, animals and mythological figures elsewhere on the canvas. For the first time, da Vinci depicted what existed beneath the skin through facial expressions and body postures captured in luminous detail — thus, Mona Lisa has become emblematic of feminine mystique and the secret behind her enigmatic smile has fuelled reams of research.

Other Endeavours

Though da Vinci is best known for his artistic masterpieces, his creative genius extended to science and technology as well. He designed military machines like the armoured car, which can be considered the precursor to the modern tank, and invented movable bridges and ladders as well as weapons like the triple-barrelled gun. To him goes the credit of designing the earliest prototypes of many aerial machines like the 'Flying Machine' or 'ornithopter', the 'airscrew' presaging the modern-day helicopter and even a triangular predecessor of the spherical parachute. Considering the military requirements of the water city of Venice, he even designed scuba gear for soldiers to execute underwater sneak attacks on enemy ships. Among other fascinating designs that have been discovered from his journals is a self-propelled cart which not only anticipates a modern motor car, but a driverless one, too! Yet another prescient design is that of a robotic knight filled with gears and wheels, connected to an elaborate pulley-and-cable system that made it capable of independent motion. All this proves what incredibly varied skills and talents da Vinci possessed—the ideal Renaissance man who was knowledgeable about multiple disciplines and never stopped pushing their boundaries.

Death and Legacy

Da Vinci spent the final years of his life under the patronage of French Emperor François I. The king not only offered him a permanent position as 'first painter and engineer' of the French Royal Court but also lasting regard and companionship. It is believed that on 2 May 1519, da Vinci breathed his last in the arms of François I—an image that has been immortalized in the 1818 painting by Jean Auguste Dominique Ingres, titled François I Receives the Last Breaths of Leonardo da Vinci. With this was lost to the world a true Renaissance polymath, an artist who pioneered the exquisite Realist style of painting and popularized techniques like sfumato, perspective and chiaroscuro. Centuries later, many of his ideas and designs would be given practical shape, proving him to be a man clearly far ahead of his time.

Trivia

- Salvator Mundi was sold for a staggering US$ 450.3 million dollars at an auction in 2017.
- Despite designing so many aerial, military and automated machines, not a single one was invented during his lifetime.
- In 2006, Italy's Institute and Museum of the History of Science in Florence built a working model of a self-propelled cart based on da Vinci's design and, incredibly, it actually worked.
- Da Vinci's designs are to be found in outer space as well—robotics expert Mark Rosheim applied some of da Vinci's ideas to the design of robots for planetary exploration, which were eventually used by NASA!

2. Michelangelo di Lodovico Buonarroti Simoni

With him, the rich artistic imagination is expressed with brilliant technical finesse. The colours are vivid and at the same time harmoniously combined; the forms are meticulously natural and the lines faithful to science of perspective even as the whole work is lit up with an inner radiance. All hardly surprising — since the artist is the Renaissance icon, Michelangelo. Sculptor, painter, poet and architect, Michelangelo was the quintessential Renaissance man, skilled in varied arts and sciences. His paintings and sculptures, executed with fine realism and classical dignity, have long been held up as the pinnacle of high Renaissance art and went on to inspire generations of artists in Europe and beyond.

Early Life and Work

What we know about Michelangelo today comes from two biographies written during his lifetime—a novelty in those days. One was written by Giorgio Vasari and the other, apparently authorized by Michelangelo himself, was written by his assistant Ascanio Condivi.

Born as Michelangelo Buonarroti on 6 March 1475 at Caprese in the then Republic of Florence, the future artist grew up in comfortable circumstances since his father held a minor administrative post in the government. At thirteen years of age, Michelangelo was apprenticed to the most famous artist in Florence at the time, Domenico Ghirlandaio. Back then, it was common for apprentices to draw copies of their master's paintings. Several such copies of Ghirlandaio as well as older Florentine painters such as Giotto di Bondone and Masaccio (born as Tommaso di Ser Giovanni di Simone) have survived through Michelangelo's hands.

Michelangelo's first masterpiece dates back to this phase. Titled The Torment of Saint Anthony, this painting is based on an engraving by fifteenth-century German painter and printmaker Martin Schongauer. Though guided by his older friend Francesco Granacci, Michelangelo was probably just twelve or thirteen years old when he created this work.

MICHELANGELO DI LODOVICO BUONARROTI SIMONI

Early Art

In the latter half of fifteenth century, the reigning Medici family of Florence was a great patron of arts and culture. However, increasing political tumult towards the end of 1480s and the eventual overthrow of the Medicis in 1494 led to many artists leaving Florence for better working conditions. Michelangelo was one of them—he first travelled to Bologna and then, after a brief return to Florence, arrived in Rome. During this time, he worked mainly as a sculptor and the first large statue that he created was Bacchus, circa 1496–97. This was followed by a commission from a French Cardinal, Jean de Bilhères, of a statue depicting the lamentation of Mother Mary for Jesus after his crucifixion. The theme—called Pieta—was common for funereal tombs of the time but in the hands of Michelangelo, the statue emerged as a work of exquisite naturalism and emotion, evocative of a mother's profound but restrained sorrow. This was also the only artwork that Michelangelo signed.

Other famous sculptures given shape by Michelangelo in the early years of 1500s were the Madonna of Bruges as well as David, the work which immortalized him. The statue is as remarkable for its depiction of masculine physical perfection as for the expression of tension in the figure's alert muscles as he is about to face an enemy on the battlefield.

The Sistine Chapel

Michelangelo was an established sculptor by the time Pope Julius II approached him to paint the ceiling of the Sistine Chapel. He started the work in 1508 and for the next four years would painstakingly bring to life as many as nine biblical stories from the *Book of Genesis*. The first three took the Creation of the World for their theme, the next three illustrated stories of Adam and Eve, and the remaining three dealt with the stories of Noah. That was not all—below these scenes from Genesis were the figures of prophets and sibyls and then, starting with Abraham, depictions of forty generations of Christ's ancestors. When complete, the fresco was as magnificent in scope as it was brilliant in its minute details. Like all true artists, Michelangelo fused his innovations with commissioned themes. For example, instead of following the artistic convention of the time to paint holy figures in frescoes, he gave the central space to dramatic scenes and decorated the sides with figures. Also, with growing assurance of his artistic ability, Michelangelo began eschewing stylistic conventions like initial drawings and preparatory incisions. The figures, as in the majestic Creation of Adam, show a fluidity of movement and harmony of colours never seen till then. Towards the end, his figures depict psychological complexities like emotions of stress and pain, as in the painting of the prophet Jonah. All this makes the ceiling of the Sistine Chapel the epitome of High Renaissance art.

Other Creations

The only known surviving panel painted by Michelangelo is titled Doni Tondo, finished just before he received the Sistine Chapel commission. Starting with the beautifully ornate wooden piece designed by the painter himself to the vivid hues and unusual pose of the Holy Family, the work has enough to anticipate the artistic innovations that would reach full flowering on the ceiling of the Sistine Chapel.

Soon after Michelangelo finished work on the Sistine Chapel, he returned to the medium he thought of as his core art—sculpture. From 1513 to 1515, he worked on a marble statue of Moses that was commissioned as early as 1505 by Pope Julius II for his funeral monument, but could be completed only after the cardinal's death. Apart from Michelangelo's poetry with chisel, the statue is also interesting for its depiction of Moses with a pair of horns.

The new Pope Leo X not only emerged as one of Michelangelo's trusted patrons, he also encouraged the artist to explore other avenues such as architecture and designing. As a result, Michelangelo directed the interiors of Medici Chapel including its allegorical sculptures—Day, Night, Dusk and Dawn, the Laurentian Library and military fortifications for the Medicis.

In 1534, Michelangelo left Florence for Rome, where he had been invited to work on varied projects. His growing professional fame and assistance left him with more leisure, evident in the poetry that survives from this phase in his life. There are at least three hundred poems including seventy-five sonnets and ninety-five madrigals (a type of song in which several singers sing different notes) on themes ranging from love—both human and spiritual—to the increasingly pressing one of mortality and legacy.

The Last Judgement

Almost twenty-five years after he had painted its ceiling, Michelangelo returned to the Sistine Chapel to paint The Last Judgment on its end wall. The awe-inspiring work depicting God's final judgment of humankind was different from Michelangelo's earlier fresco in many ways. Instead of the detailing and attractive naturalism evident in his previous paintings, Michelangelo's later work has simpler but more contrasted colour schemes—like the flesh tones standing out against the deep blue sky. However, The Last Judgment shows as much complexity as the former fresco, especially in its depiction of emotional intensity, like in the cries and expressions of the people receiving the judgment.

Death

Michelangelo's last fresco was The Crucifixion of St. Peter, completed in 1550. The statues and poems of his final years would echo the same concern with impending death and mortality. On 18 February 1564, Michelangelo died in Rome, barely three weeks from his eighty-eighth birthday.

Trivia

- Michelangelo was the first artist to have his life chronicled during his own lifetime—not once but twice.
- Initially apprenticed for a three-year term to Ghirlandaio, young Michelangelo left after the first year since, according to his biographer Condivi, there was nothing more that the older painter could teach his precocious student.
- In 1972, Hungarian-born Australian geologist Lazlo Toth attacked Michelangelo's most evocative sculpture, Pieta, with a hammer.
- At the time of its painting, the iconic The Last Judgment was met with severe disapproval from the Vatican due to nudity.

3. Rembrandt Harmenszoon van Rijn

Supremely skilful handling of light and texture, intense emotional insight into subjects as well as finely detailed landscapes—these are the hallmarks of Rembrandt. He was a towering figure of the Dutch Golden Age, during which arts and culture, fuelled by lucrative trade and commerce, thrived in this small country. Rembrandt would come to be associated with the Baroque style of art that sought to convey, through rich sensual imagery, the drama of human emotions and existence. Handling a variety of themes and styles with consummate skill, Rembrandt continues to be regarded as one of the most accomplished painters of all times.

Early Life

Born Rembrandt Harmenszoon van Rijn on 15 July 1606 at

Leiden, Netherlands, into a miller's family, the future artist received a conventional school education which included extensive Biblical and Christian stories—these would go on to make up many of his artistic themes in adult years.

From 1620 to 1624-25, Rembrandt served as an apprentice to two masters—Jacob van Swanenburgh and Pieter Lastman. The latter was an established painter of the historical genre—a particularly popular genre in those times, in which famous biblical, historical, mythological or allegorical characters would be placed in complex settings. Other artists who influenced Rembrandt were Jan Lievens and Jacob Pynas.

Early Art

After completing his apprenticeship, Rembrandt settled in Leiden in 1625 as an independent painter. During those times, it was common for new painters to take their masters' established paintings and create their own variations—something that Rembrandt did with Lastman's historical themes. However, in the paintings of this time such as Raising of Lazarus, Judas Repentant and The Artist in His Studio, it is clear that Rembrandt was recomposing conventional themes, especially playing with exotic settings and costumes—all traits of another popular contemporary sub-genre of paintings known as Tronies.

Technical Artistry

Towards the end of the 1620s, there came about a distinct change in Rembrandt's style. He now began using light in a different way—concentrating on its source and then expanding its impact to create a spotlight-like effect, complemented by the shadowy areas of the composition. The 1628 painting Peter and Paul Disputing displays this technique as well as his system of 'bevriende kleuren', which involved grouping closely related colours in certain places of the canvas, especially the foreground. The effect was two-fold—achieving a highly illuminated area as well as providing unity to the composition.

In 1631, Rembrandt decided to move to Amsterdam and would eventually join its St Luke Guild in 1634. Before that he entered into a partnership with Hendrick van Uylenburgh, in whose workshop Rembrandt began painting. Later, he would also marry Uylenburgh's niece Saskia. This was the heyday of portraiture, both individual and group. Dutch traders, flush with commercial success, would want their portraits painted, often in oriental settings and costumes, while guilds would commission group portraits of their work, achievements and members. An example of individual portraiture would be Man in Oriental Costume (1632), which is remarkable for its light effects and depth, achieved as much by dextrous golden highlights as by a limited colour palette. To the tradition of group portraits belongs one of Rembrandt's best works of this phase, The Anatomy Lesson of Dr Nicolaes Tulp (1632), which was based on the then annual practice of holding an anatomy session in January – attended not only by academicians and students of the university but also general ticket-purchasing public. The most important parts of the composition – the cadaver, the faces of the students, and Dr Tulp's hands – are illuminated and contrasted by the dark colours of the students' robes. The scene is highly dramatic – though also brilliantly unified by the angle and line of the dead body, taking the viewer to the centre of the composition.

Growing Fame

Rembrandt continued to paint Biblical, historical and mythological themes, though with far greater artistic skill than before. For example, in The Storm on the Sea of Galilee (1633), the brightly lit frothing waves are a stark reminder of the danger the boat is in. The sense of fear and drama are heightened by the expressions of the people in peril, including the one who looks directly at the viewer, whom critics have interpreted as Rembrandt himself (he would often paint himself into his compositions). Among his 'Old Testament' scenes are Bathsheba at Her Bath and Jacob Blessing the Sons of Joseph. Danae is one of Rembrandt's few mythological paintings and his supreme handling of light in the painting literally illustrates the theme as well. Danae, the daughter of King Akrisios, is isolated to prevent the fulfilment a prophecy that her son would kill Danae's father. However, Zeus appears to her as a ray of golden light and out of the union is born Perseus who eventually grows up and kills Akrisios.

One of Rembrandt's best-known masterpieces, The Night Watch, is also an example of a group portrait commissioned by a guild—this time by the rather wealthy one of the civic militias. The painting is as rich with professional and social details as with technical brilliance like the play of light and shadows. It is also animated by a sense of movement and bustle. Indeed, it is a mark of Rembrandt's artistic innovation that instead of depicting the guild members in formal pose, he placed them in the thick of action.

Later Phase

Art historians have noted a decline in Rembrandt's output from the mid-1640s onwards. Several theories have been put forward to explain this, ranging from depression at the death of his wife to the rejection of commissioned works and resulting debts. Critics now largely agree that the popularity of French classicism in Dutch art in the mid-seventeenth century may have caused Rembrandt to slow down. However, his paintings from the later phase of his artistic life depict a keener psychological insight. Among his forty-odd self-portraits painted across his career, The Self-Portrait with Two Circles stands out for its meticulous detail that refuses either to sentimentalize or idealize the subject. At the same time, the image of two circles—conventionally symbolizing perfection—in the flat, plain background is perhaps the artist's way of taking pride in his artistic skills. Another masterpiece from the later part of his career was The Jewish Bride (1665) depicting a couple—popularly interpreted as the Old Testament patriarch Isaac and his wife Rebecca—in a moment of gentle and affectionate intimacy.

The last paintings by Rembrandt were created as part of a partnership with his son Titus and his common-law wife Heindriche. In 1669, Rembrandt died and was buried in an unmarked grave.

Legacy

Rembrandt's artistic genius lay in his wide-ranging skills. He was the master of close naturalism as well as the play of light and shade. While he took traditional subjects like Biblical and mythological figures as well as individual and group portraits as his themes, Rembrandt was perhaps the first Western painter to imbue them with emotional intensity and psychological depth. He also used myriad materials to express his artistic genius. Apart from paintings, Rembrandt left behind masterly sketches and etchings which number at more than three hundred. In fact, he was more famous internationally for the prints based on his etchings. Rembrandt was not only widely copied by his own students and painters of his time but would go on to leave a stronger influence on generations of artistic icons such as Vincent Van Gogh. '...Rembrandt goes so deep into the mysterious that he says things for which there are no words in any language. It is justice that they call him Rembrandt—magician,' he would say about the Dutch Master.

Trivia

- During the peak of his career, Rembrandt taught students painting and charged an annual tuition fee of 100 guilders (old Dutch currency).
- His most famous painting, The Night Watch, is set during the day.
- Rembrandt painted himself in many of his works, like The Stoning of St. Stephen, The Storm at Sea, The Raising of the Cross and perhaps even in The Night Watch.

4. Johannes Vermeer

The paint glows with a luminosity that makes the viewer want to reach out, half-expecting the fingers to touch a real pearl. The play of light and shade is of the utmost delicacy while the lines are finely drawn, all lending an amazing level of realism to the paintings. This is the art for which Johannes Vermeer is still revered — some six hundred years after he captured a series of domestic as well as outdoor scenes of his beloved Dutch life. Though he left behind just thirty-six paintings, each is a valued masterpiece today, not just for its breathtaking artistry but for depiction of the quiet and comfortable dignity of the lives of ordinary Dutch folk.

Early Life and Work

There is no reliable record of his date of birth, though it is certain that Johannes Vermeer was baptized on

31 October 1632 at the place of his birth, Delft, in the Netherlands. Young Johannes grew up in comfort, since his father was a skilled weaver and an art dealer. With the creative spirit already in his genes, Johannes was able to pick up artistic skills from other masters in the Delft guild as well as in Utrecht where he may have ventured after his marriage to a Catholic girl named Catherine Bolnes and his conversion to Catholicism.

The Utrecht school of painting, at that time, was deeply influenced by the religious themes of Caravaggio and his style of using lamps and fires for artificial lighting. All this influenced Vermeer's early work, like Christ in the House of Mary and Martha as well as Diana and Her Nymphs, which shows the impact of religious and mythological subjects. The other significant influence on Vermeer at this time was fellow Dutch painter Rembrandt from whom he picked up the use of chiaroscuro which gave his subjects a psychological intensity. An early masterpiece that gives evidence of such influence is a 1656 painting titled The Procuress. Here, the theme of love for money is as far removed from the prevalent themes like divine love as is Vermeer's growing individualism from his earlier imitative style. The vibrant colours and rich tapestry of the rug seem to set the canvas aflame in contrast to the male figures in shadows, indicating their moral ambiguity.

Middle Phase

Other contemporary Dutch painters like Gerard Terborsch and Carel Fabritius—who was also Rembrandt's pupil—too influenced Vermeer. As a result, from late 1650s, he moved away from large-scale mythological themes to smaller, cosier depictions of everyday life in Dutch homes and landscapes. Girl Reading a Letter at an Open Window (circa 1657) is rich in technical artistry like the rendering of the sun's rays streaming in from the open window. Evidence of his experimenting with the technique of illusionism is seen in the way he has painted the girl's reflection on the window pane. At the same time, they evoke feelings of an easy quietude and a cherished privacy with none of the angst of solitude—all that Vermeer's paintings would become famous for.

Another painter from this time by whom Vermeer may have been influenced was Pieter de Hooch. Though there is no historical evidence showing that these two knew each other personally, Vermeer may well have got from Hooch's own work—especially the courtyard paintings—the idea of using perspective to depict a space like a room or part of a street filled with light. Also, the figures situated in such spaces exude a sense of comfortable domesticity and familiar ease in their surroundings. All these qualities are to be found in the View of Houses in Delft that Vermeer painted around

1658 and which also came to be known as The Little Street.

Period of Artistic Maturity

As Vermeer's art grew in confidence and technical dexterity, his name commanded increased influence. In 1662, Vermeer was nominated the head of the painters' guild in his home town. For the rest of his life, his artwork would find regular buyers from among a small but wealthy group of patrons based in Delft.

The best of his artwork belong to these years in the middle of Vermeer's career. Paintings like Young Woman with a Water Pitcher (circa 1662), Woman with a Pearl Necklace (circa 1662/65), and Woman in Blue Reading a Letter (circa 1663) usually depict interior scenes of everyday comfortable domesticity. Subjects are usually women—going about their daily chores or indulging in leisure activities like practising music and sometimes lost in private thought, reading or writing letters. The remarkable thing about these subjects is that Vermeer does not invest them with any larger narrative or striking symbolism. Objects depicted within the canvas like chairs, tables, walls, maps, and window frames do not bear any burden of the painter's personal symbolism and yet their arrangement is never random. Vermeer's careful eye inevitably painted objects in a way that their lines, colours, proportions and placement would harmonize with the central subject. And over everything glimmers the play of light and shade that not only gives evidence of his acute Realist technique but indeed unifies the composition in a highly aesthetic way.

An especially remarkable example of such harmony of effect is the 1664 painting Woman Holding a Balance where every element of the painting—from the serenity of the subject's expression to the harmony of colours and forms in the room seem to be represented by the evenness of scales with which she is weighing the precious stones. Critics have found philosophical depth in this painting based on the religious painting, The Last Judgment, the background of which seems to suggest that every action will have its own reaction in the afterlife or perhaps that material success as symbolized by the gems should be balanced with religious faith. But overall, Vermeer desisted from strident symbolism and focused more on conveying a sense of dignity, even when depicting ordinary folk going about their daily chores.

Technical Brilliance

Vermeer also brought this loving familiarity into his landscapes, of which View of Delft (circa 1660–61) is considered among his best. This depicts a view of Delft from across its harbour and its iconic structures like the tower of the Nieuwe Kerk, the huge city gates and walls. The painting conveys a sense of massive substance by its depiction of big buildings gates and walls, and at the same time, is illuminated by Vermeer's signature radiant effect achieved by juxtaposing small dots of unmodulated colours with touches of the brush. Other paintings in which this style leads to breathtaking detail of objects in the foreground are the crusty bread in The Milkmaid (circa 1658) as well as the chair decorations in Girl with a Red Hat (circa 1665/66). This painting is also held up by art historians like Charles Seymour as evidence of another stylistic innovation of the times—the use of the camera obscura. This was a camera-like device marked by limited depth of field. As a result, the projected image had several unfocused areas, edged by diffused highlights. These optical effects may have fascinated Vermeer and the characteristic soft focus of his subjects could have been due to the use of camera obscura. However, not all art historians agree on Vermeer's use of camera obscura in his paintings.

What instead seems more remarkable about the detailed realism of Vermeer's paintings is the almost mathematical precision of perspective. Art critics like Joseph Pennell have pointed this out in Vermeer's paintings like Officer and Laughing Girl, describing it as 'photographic perspective' of Vermeer. The vanishing point of the perspective is yet another technique which he used with extreme skill to emphasize the main compositional element in the painting—for example, in Woman Holding a Balance, this point of vanishing perspective is marked by the fingertip of the woman's hand in which she holds the balance, as though to drive home the theme and effect of measure and harmony.

When compared to the intense subjectivity of many painters of this time, Vermeer comes across as rather self-effacing. He lacks the obsession with self-portraits and does not project personal symbols on the canvas. However, in The Art of Painting (circa 1666/68), he gave a glimpse of what he thought of his own creative pursuit. The subject is a rather wealthy artist painting the allegorical character of Clio—the Muse of History who is depicted with her characteristic laurel wreath, trumpet and heavy book. This, together with the map in the background, suggests that Vermeer considered art to be a significant expression of the history of a time, place and his own people.

Later Life and Art

Later in his life, Vermeer began exploring the atmospheric possibilities of his themes rather than focusing on figures or portraits. The style too is less diffused—the brushstrokes appear to be tighter, the lines more angular and use of colour much bolder. These features are marked in later paintings like Lady Writing a Letter with Her Maid (1670) and The Guitar Player (circa 1672).

Though Vermeer was elected the head of the Delft painting guild again in 1670, his fortunes fell soon after due to the slump in Dutch economy following the French invasion of 1672. Three years later, in December 1675, Vermeer, overcome by debt and illness, breathed his last in the city of his birth and work, Delft.

Trivia

- The artwork titled The Art of Painting was so important to Vermeer that his widow tried to save it from creditors even when the family desperately needed money.
- As the number of paintings Vermeer made in his lifetime was small, his work was especially vulnerable to forgeries—the most infamous copier being Han van Van Meegeren who passed as many as fourteen of his own paintings under Vermeer's name.
- Vermeer's painting Girl with a Pearl Earring has inspired a novel by Tracy Chevalier as well as a film based on the novel, starring Scarlett Johansson and Colin Firth.

5. Peter Paul Rubens

The colours and details glow with a sensory richness while the lines and shapes flow with a spontaneous charm. The play of light and shade illuminates the sensous forms, thus giving rise to the adjective 'Rubenesque' and leading to the high point of the Baroque style. The artist responsible for such extravagance of imagination, technique and energy was none other than the seventeenth, century Flemish painter, Peter Paul Rubens. Rubens' life and career represented the happy fusion of professional and artistic success. He presided over a large studio where he created his art, which also included a busy workshop that was frequented by apprentices, artists and collectors. Rejecting the austerity of the Reformation, he not only imagined the world as bursting with light, colours and textures but ensured that his art was rewarded with fame and success.

Early Life

Born on 28 June 1577 at Siegen, Nassau, in present-day Germany to a Calvinist father, Peter Paul Rubens moved to Antwerp, Belgium, only a few years after his father's death. There, he was brought up in the Roman Catholic culture of his mother's family and received a classical education—influences which probably led to the dominance of Christian and mythological themes in his paintings. After being apprenticed to moderately skilled painters a couple of times, he finally got as his master, Otto van Veen, the most famous artist in Antwerp at the time, who was also the dean of the painters' guild of St. Luke.

Early Art

In 1598, Rubens was accepted into the painters' guild in Antwerp but after a couple of years, he left for Italy where he must have come across the dramatic intensity in the best of Renaissance art by Masters like Titian, Tintoretto and Veronese. Rubens also absorbed all the glamour, pageantry and exuberance of court life during his professional tours across Italy. In 1601, he finally arrived in Rome where the new Baroque style had begun to appear in the works of Caravaggio and Carracci. With his background of classical education and artistic training in Flemish realism, the style naturally came to Rubens and his imagination was inflamed by courtly grandeur. Even as he was commissioned to paint Renaissance-style portraits for court officials, his innate affability and level-headedness led to him being sent as a diplomat to Spain to present a shipment of paintings to King Philip III. For the king's prime minister, the Duke of Lerma, Rubens painted a portrait (1603) which is now considered among his earliest masterpieces. The depiction of physical traits like the muscularity of the horse and the stature of its rider convey a sense of power and majesty while details like the glittering armour, the delicacy of the ruff and the shining mane of the horse gleam with the richness of the Baroque style.

Rubens' self-portrait with Isabella Brant, his first wife, titled Honeysuckle Bower (1609) adopts a similar style and reveals his growing professional success. Rubens had already got a prestigious commission in 1606 to paint the altarpiece of Chiesa Nuova or the Church of Santa Maria in Vallicella, Italy, and upon his return to Antwerp, he was asked to paint a celebratory Adoration of the Magi (1609) for the Antwerp Town Hall. The fame brought by this commission enabled Rubens to get married in October that year and buy a big house, which was soon expanded to include a classical portico, garden walks and most importantly, a sprawling studio.

Growing Fame

The 'Twelve Years Truce' ushered in a wave of Counter-Reformation revival of art and culture in Belgium. This was a time when churches and chapels, freed from the starkness of Reformation, would commission elaborate religious art like triptychs (a picture in three panels) and altarpieces. From 1610–1614, Rubens painted two triptychs titled Raising of the Cross and Descent from the Cross. The Great Last Judgement and Christ on the Cross, also called Le Coup de Lance, are among other religious masterpieces by Rubens from this period. A particularly remarkable work by the painter is Massacre of the Innocents in which the gut-wrenching expression of sorrow of mothers at the death of their children is underlined with intense dramatic action. However, the artist's most famous theme appears to be Adoration of the Magi depicted in at least twelve of his paintings.

At the same time, Rubens continued to use classical themes like in the Rape of the Daughters of Leucippus, Prometheus Bound and The Hippopotamus and Crocodile Hunt to give brilliant expression to the voluptuous fervour of his Baroque art. Despite the popularity of figures, Rubens also mastered landscape painting as evident in the works titled The Four Continents, The Lion Hunt and Landscape with Craters. A fusion of historical event and mythological setting is seen in The Disembarkation at Marseilles in which the arrival of Madame de' Medici to marry the French King Henry IV is celebrated with mythological figures—such as Poseidon and his three daughters—in attendance. Rubens would go on to paint twenty-one canvases for her, depicting her life and regency in France in epic grandeur. This belonged to the tradition of tapestry paintings, usually commissioned by royals and high-ranked nobles, of which Rubens painted several.

Later Phase

As if art did not keep him busy enough, Rubens, in the second half of 1620s, began working as a diplomat as well, trying to negotiate a peace treaty between England and Spain. These efforts found artistic expression in Peace and War (1629–30).

When he returned to Antwerp in 1631, Rubens got back to painting with a renewed vigour, brought upon partly by his marriage to sixteen-year-old Helena Fourment. Her youth and beauty probably found its way in the sensuous imagery of paintings like Venus and Adonis, The Garden of Love, The Feast of Venus and The Kermesse. These paintings not only share the themes of love, joy, dance and music but also follow a style which is looser, more sweeping, and intent on evoking moods and textures.

Busy as Rubens was till his later years with designing arches and parades for courtly occasions, his personal art now showed a certain shift towards landscape. This is evident in works like Landscape with Rainbow (1636) and A View of Het Steen in the Early Morning (1636) which depict a rather idealized natural setting, where all creatures live in order and harmony. Towards the end of his life, Rubens painted two important self-portraits— one a rather formal Self-Portrait in 1636 and the other with his young wife and their youngest son, completed in 1640. This was probably the artist's way of underlining his legacy as a family man and professional success, before he breathed his last in 1641.

Legacy

Rubens left behind an astonishing amount and variety in artistic styles, themes, material and collaboration. He worked with an amazing energy and speed, completing commissions for royal, courtly, religious and individual clients even as he painted and designed for his personal satisfaction. Glowing colours, intricate details, sensory wealth and brilliant illumination marked the highest achievements of the Baroque style. His art inspired contemporary painters such as Van Dyck, Murillo and Rembrandt, as well as later Impressionists such as Renoir. At the same time, his business and diplomatic acumen ensured that art was a viable profession, and hence, a real career option for generations of artists to come.

Trivia

- Not surprisingly for a painter in such high demand, Rubens once described himself as 'the busiest and most harassed man in the world'.
- Rubens was knighted not once but twice — the first time in 1630 by King Charles I of England for designing the ceiling of the royal Banqueting House, and the very next year by Philip IV of Spain.

6. Katsushika Hokusai

The delicate strokes and simple colours on the screen paintings bring to life the beauty of courtesans and kabuki actors. On the other hand, the flowers and figures in the later paintings amaze with their intricate details. This trajectory belongs to master artist and printmaker, Katsushika Hokusai, who developed a new artistic sensibility in Japan — a fusion of traditional strokes and Western realism.

Early Life

Born in October 1760 in the eastern quarter of Edo, now Tokyo, Hokusai apparently started drawing as early as the age of five. He received early training from Nakajima, a reputed mirror maker, whose household he was brought up in. But since Hokusai did not become an heir, historians have surmised that he must have been Nakajima's child from a concubine. Working as a clerk in a bookstore in his early youth, Hokusai became interested in woodcut prints, and for three years, apprenticed with a woodblock engraver. All this would eventually contribute to his mastery and innovation of woodcut prints.

Early Art

To learn more, Hokusai became the student of Katsukawa Shunshō, the leading artist of the ukiyo-e tradition. This was a form of art which involved making drawings, paintings and prints of the leisure world then, including those of courtesans, kabuki theatre, its actors and so on. For almost a decade, Hokusai worked in Shunshō's studio, producing woodcut prints under the name Shunro, given by his master. During this time, he married twice and had children. To support his growing family, Hokusai began working within the entire ukiyo-e spectrum, coming up with illustrations for books, verse anthologies, erotic literature and surinomo as well. The surinomo sub-genre included prints made for special purposes like announcements of music programmes or cultural events, invites from wealthy families or greetings on New Year, and similar occasions. Surinomo prints demanded high precision and expertise in the finest techniques.

Pushing Boundaries

When his master died in 1793, Hokusai began exploring other artistic styles and was drawn to the European conventions through copper engravings by the French and Dutch artists. This, as well as his studies at a rival Kato school, led Shunkō, the new chief of the Katsukawa school, to expel Hokusai. The painter, though, saw the incident as propelling him to more promising and dynamic artistic avenues, about which he said, 'What really motivated the development of my artistic style was the embarrassment I suffered at Shunkō's hands.'

A new phase in Hokusai's art was evident in his change of subject—he now began taking daily scenes of common urban life as well as landscapes as his themes. He also began employing Western artistic conventions like perspective and a diverse colour palette, and in the process, Hokusai not only emerged as a more innovative painter but widened the scope of ukiyo-e art as well. During this time, Hokusai published two collections of landscapes, Famous Sights of the Eastern Capital and Eight Views of Edo.

Growing Popularity

From the early nineteenth century, another change became evident in Hokusai's themes. With the popularity of extended historical novels known as *yomihon*, the illustrations he made now focused on classical subjects like ancient heroes, traditional characters and samurai. He also began taking on students and their number reached fifty in his lifetime.

The Phase of Maturity

To shore up his income, Hokusai, from 1812 onwards, began designing woodcut prints for artists' manuals, then known as *etehon*. The first collection titled *Quick Lessons in Simplified Drawing* was published in 1812. These soon became popular as Hokusai manga which, apart from art sketches, also included caricatures and what we would today understand as fun cartoons of people, animals and public figures. In fact, the origin of the modern Japanese manga can be traced to these popular art manuals by Hokusai of which he published as many as twelve volumes before 1820.

During the 1820s, Hokusai reached the pinnacle of his artistic fame. His best-known artwork, 36 Views of Mount Fuji, dates from this period and includes the globally recognized Great Wave off Kanagawa. With the prints doing brisk business, Hokusai added ten more prints to the series. In the same vein, he produced other series of prints titled A Tour of the Waterfalls of the Provinces and Unusual Views of Celebrated Bridges in the Provinces. Later, he would return to his beloved Mount Fuji and complete One Hundred Views of Mount Fuji during the mid-1830s.

Later Phase

Towards the end of his career, Hokusai's artistic oeuvre extended from sweeping landscape prints to intricately detailed paintings of flowers and birds. The most famous artworks of the latter group include *Poppies, Lilies* and *Flock of Chickens*.

The 1840s marked the waning of Hokusai's influence. In 1839, a fire engulfed Hokusai's studio, destroying much of his work. Eventually, the work of emerging artists like Andō Hiroshige overshadowed Hokusai's though he kept painting well into his late eighties—his exquisitely created *Ducks in a Stream* was completed when he was 87.

On 18 April 1849, Hokusai breathed his last and was buried at the Seikyō-ji in Tokyo. Even on his deathbed, he reportedly said, 'If only Heaven will give me just another ten years... Just another five more years, then I could become a real painter.' These are the words of a supreme artist who is forever in search for better styles and vision.

Legacy

Hokusai's artistic career spanned seven long decades during which he created screen paintings, prints, text illustrations, prints for private circulation, art manuals, sketches and many other forms of art. His early works represented the high point of art genres like ukiyo-e which he expanded to include varied themes and subjects. With the opening of Japan to westerners from 1853, Hokusai's prints and paintings were viewed by the rest of the world and even become an important influence in modernist art.

Trivia

- Hokusai was a consummate publicist; he would often create enormous paintings—as big as 200 square metres—in front of festive crowds and occasionally before the Shogun (a military ruler) too.
- One such public painting involved Hokusai painting a blue curve on paper and then leaving a chicken with feet dipped in red paint to scurry across the paper. He later interpreted the painting as a landscape depicting the Tatsuta River with red maple leaves floating in it!
- Hokusai's youngest daughter O-ei also became an artist and in his old age, carried on Hokusai's painting tradition.
- During his lifetime, Hokusai acquired thirty different names and changed more than ninety houses. Towards the end, he even painted under the name of 'Gakyō Rōjin Manji' which translates to 'The Old Man Mad about Art'.

7. Claude Monet

The canvas seems awash with the glimmer of natural light and exudes the fresh air in which it has taken shape. It appears to glow with the 'light and air which vary continually' — these words are a key pointer to the artistic style of one of greatest painters of the twentieth century, Claude Monet, who saw the world not as made up of realistic details and commonplace forms but as qualified by the 'surrounding atmosphere' which he claimed 'gives subjects their true value'.

Early Life

Monet was born on 14 November 1840 in Paris, but when he was five, his family moved to the Normandy coast, near Le Havre, where his father took charge of a successful grocery business. The change in setting would sow the seeds of artistic sensibility in young Monet as he would see the seascape change colour and mood in various seasons and times of the day. Soon, Monet was drawing pencil sketches of ships and boats on the Norman coast, even managing to draw and sell a series of caricatures of local people when he was just fifteen years old.

Monet's aunt, Marie-Jeanne Lecadre, was an amateur painter and she realized that the budding artist could do with some formal instruction. But while young Monet studied drawing under a local artist, French painter Eugène Boudin was a greater influence in these early years. This painter persuaded young Monet to step out of the confines of the indoor studio into open air to capture his subject amidst the varying effects of light and air. This was quite an unconventional idea at the time but Monet took to it instinctively.

To soak all the innovations in the world of art, Monet lived in Paris from 1859 to 1860, and after that, he left to Algeria for military service. This, too, would enrich his future artistic life by exposing him to more colourful landscapes and outdoors.

Early Art

To some extent Monet's early art was also influenced by Realists who believed in depicting a subject in all its physical particularity, neither idealizing it nor imbuing it with personal significance, and the effect can be seen in Luncheon on the Grass painted sometime in 1865–66. Similarly, Women in the Garden depicts the effects of outdoor light, rejecting the artistic conventions of formal poses or models surrounded by drapery. By the time paintings like The Beach at Sainte-Adresse (1867) and On the Bank of the Seine, Bennecourt (1868) came about, Monet was already showing glimpses of moving away from the Realist to the Impressionist world with his looser brushstrokes and more vivid colouring.

Impressionist Style

The paintings of the 1870s, like Westminster Bridge and Boulevard des Capucines reveal a surer grasp of his new technique. In these paintings, Monet was trying not so much to recreate exactly the seascapes and landscapes before him as trying to give an impression of how the scene appeared in that moment—in that particular natural light, in the movement of people or objects, in the blowing breeze, in the gathering mist. Thus, objects and figures are not detailed but finished in a few quick strokes—the sky, waves, mist and beach are depicted in their shifting, liquid atmosphere. This was a highly innovative style at that time and attracted other young painters like Frédéric Bazille, Alfred Sisley, Pierre-Auguste Renoir, Camille Pissarro and others. These painters put up an independent exhibition of their works in 1874, which displayed Monet's Impression,

Sunrise (1872). This led art journalist Louis Leroy to mock the group as 'Impressionists', but the title was embraced with fervour by the artists and soon it was being widely used to describe their distinctive style.

Monet's focus on the effects of natural light are especially evident in paintings of figures like Woman with a Parasol, depicting his wife and son in the background. Typically, the faces are hazy or shadowed while the painting is more interesting in how the light falls on the grass and is reflected in the sky, and everything is animated by the blowing wind. The Rue Montorgueil in Paris, Celebration of June 30th, 1878, and Rouen Cathedral: The Facade at Sunset are other examples of Monet's keen interest in visual perception, especially the optics of light and movement.

Despite growing artistic finesse, the 1870s was not a happy time for Monet, personally. He was burdened by heavy financial debt and even his marriage was unravelling. Moving from one place to another, Monet arrived at Vétheuil in 1876 and found himself in a romantic affair with a woman named Alice Hoschedé who was separated from her husband. Alice paid off Monet's debts from her own dowry and even cared for his sick wife till she died in 1879.

Later Phase

After more travelling and painting, Monet finally bought a house in Giverny, a hamlet on the small Epte River, and settled there with Alice and their children in 1883.

In the new century, Monet began working on a specific series—he would choose a subject and then paint it under varied atmospheric conditions of light, mist and movement. The first of these series, comprising paintings like Waterloo Bridge, Sunlight Effect, was set in London between 1899 and 1904 and depicted the Thames River, the Waterloo and Charing Cross bridges, as well as the Houses of Parliament.

However, the series which is most associated with Monet's artistic genius is titled Water Lilies, which he painted from 1915 to 1926. This series, inspired by his own garden at Giverny, comprises dozens of huge canvases capturing different views of the lilies against a changing symphony of elements like sky and water. The final installation, displaying eight most valuable paintings in this series, was designed to reflect Monet's own ethereal vision of the series—'Imagine a circular room, whose walls are entirely filled by a horizon of water spotted with these plants...' so that the entire display gives the 'illusion of an endless whole, of a wave with no horizon and no shore'.

The Water Lilies series in fact kept Monet busy, despite

his failing eyesight and weakening health, till his death in 1926. Towards the end, his paintings seemed to crystallize the erstwhile 'impressions' into the decorative qualities of form and colour. Rather than exploring how an outdoor scene appears in varying atmospheric conditions, he later used smaller brushstrokes and almost complete blurring of figures to explore the blends and contrasts of texture and colour. In this, Monet anticipated the vivid palette of the Post-Impressionists such as Van Gogh and Cézanne as well as the abstract idiom of Expressionists, especially of the New York school, like Mark Rothko and Jackson Pollock—thus firmly establishing Monet's reputation as one of the towering figures of Modern Western Art.

Trivia

- Monet suffered from depression for most of his adult life.
- As Monet's first wife, Camille, died of uterine cancer, he captured those moments on canvas—the result was a deeply-felt painting titled Camille on Her Deathbed (1879).
- Monet hired gardeners to dust the surface of his pond before he painted it for his famous Water Lilies series.

8. Paul Cézanne

Every part of the canvas looks as though it is contributing to an overall structural harmony. The same object is depicted from multiple angles, the brushstrokes are controlled though the palette is vivid. It is as though the hand, rather than merely painting the subject, has constructed it — the artist is Post-Impressionist icon Paul Cézanne. Nicknamed the 'Master of Aix', after his hometown, Cézanne had significant influence on the abstractionist styles of painting that emerged with Expressionism and Fauvism and is particularly regarded as the precursor to Cubism.

Early Life

Born on 19 January 1839 in Aix-en-Provence, France, to a successful banker, Paul Cézanne grew up in middle-class comfort. However, this also had the result of imposing certain expectations, and in keeping with his father's desires, Cézanne initially trained to join the world of law. Around 1860, Cézanne realized that his heart lay in painting and with the support of his mother he managed to convince his father to let him leave for Paris to study art. However, the academic style of painting that was conventional at the time did not appeal to Cézanne and for a while he returned to Aix to try and work for his father's financial business.

Early Art

Till 1872, Cézanne would keep moving between Aix and Paris, trying to find an individual idiom of art. In Paris, he was greatly influenced by the radical new group of artists who were determined to break away from the romantic style of painting exemplified by Delacroix and favoured by the official Academie de Beaux-art and its Salon. These painters would go on to develop their own style and exhibition platform under Impressionism. Influenced as he was by their rejection of sentimental romanticizing of subject and attracted as he was by the realism of Courbet—a favourite of the Impressionists—Cézanne did not entirely agree with the Impressionist emphasis on atmosphere and its light brushwork. Instead, he opted for greater solidity of colour and technique and a harmony of composition—almost architectural in nature.

All these aspects are evident in Cézanne's first masterpiece—The Artist's Father, reading *L'Événement*—painted in 1866. Objects acquire symbolic overtones by indicating incompatibility—the painting in the background, possibly by Cézanne, versus the old man's stern expression; the liberalism as represented by *L'Événement* is also clearly opposed to the well-known conservatism of Cézanne's father, Louis-Auguste's ideologies. During this early phase, Cézanne's style reveals a vigour and solidity complemented by bold extremes of light and shadow as in A Modern Olympia (1873-74), sometimes leading to darker palette and brooding themes like The Abduction (1867) and The Murder (1867-68).

Impressionist Influence

In 1870, Cézanne left Paris with his mistress, Marie-Hortense Fiquet. The two arrived in Provence where Cézanne began painting landscapes. In 1886, the two married and settled at Estaque, a small village on the southern French coast. During this time, Cézanne was influenced by the Impressionist way of depicting the myriad appearances of land, sea and sky, in different conditions of light. Snow at Estaque (1870-71) and The Wine Market (1872) are some of his paintings in this style. This influence grew stronger under the influence of Camille Pissarro who Cézanne joined at Pontoise along with his family. This resulted in

Cézanne adopting a lighter palette, breaking up bits of colour and using shorter brushstrokes—all hallmarks of the Impressionist style. And yet, he believed in lending structure to the objects he painted rather than leaving them ephemeral in the impressionist way. This blending of styles is clear in The House of the Suicide (1873) and even more in The Bay of Marseille, Seen from L'Estaque painted between 1878–79,in which the bold blues of the sky and sea, the steady brushwork and the architectonic forms of the houses in the foreground give solidity and substance to the composition.

From the mid-1870s, Cézanne's situation became increasingly difficult. Lack of buyers for his paintings meant that he was still financially dependent on his father who was bitterly critical of his son's lack of material success. Both professionally and personally, Cézanne was also moving away from the Impressionist and his difficult temperament even led to an estrangement with once close friend, Emile Zola.

Later Art

'Everything in Nature is modelled after the sphere, the cone, and the cylinder. One must learn to paint from these simple figures.' This philosophy increasingly came to guide Cézanne's artistic style from the late 1880s. For example, in the The Mills of Gardanne (circa 1885), the landscape seems to be made of massive prisms, far removed from the shimmering eloquence of light of the Impressionist nature scenes. The preponderance for solidity and substance also lent his subjects—whether portraits like Madame Cézanne in a Red Dress (1888-1890) or figures like The Card Players (1890-1892)—almost a timeless quality. Rather than breathing, moving people, they appear as variations of Cézanne's favourite still life. The Card Players, in fact, was composed as a series of paintings and drawings based on the Provence locals as they went about with their usual patterns of living. Eventually, Cézanne found still life more amenable to his tendency to bring out the structural aspect of subjects, and during his career, he painted around two hundred of them. Most of them, largely painted between 1895 and 1900, were of fruits, jugs, and wine bottles on tables, all the while playing with contrasting shapes and lines. The rounded contours of apples and peaches in Table, Napkin, and Fruit (A Corner of the Table) for instance are set up in opposition to the vertical lines of tables and wooden screen in the background. The napkin not only provides the white background to set off the luscious colours of the fruits but makes them appear to float, thus further exploring possibilities of shape and space.

Cézanne's paintings from his later phase also indicate his moods and personal meanings. This, coupled with the influence of Japanese woodcut prints, made it clear that he was moving towards a more abstract style. For example, in Study of Trees (1904), he uses colour, shape and lines to achieve a harmonious blend which, rather than realistically depicting them, expresses the movement of trees. Taken literally, the composition seems to be made up of triangles and diagonal lines but the painting actually pushes beyond representational conventions to show how angles, shapes and complementary colours can express the being and indeed the vitality of the subject—in this case, the leaves which appear to be shimmering and moving on the trees. The painting is also quite typical of the incompleteness with which Fauvist style would soon come to be associated with—the purpose was to encourage the viewer to make connections, complete the picture in his/her mind and in this way, making the viewer part of the creative process.

By the time, Cézanne started painting his iconic series of Mont Sainte-Victoire near Aix, he had gained more confidence and maturity in his abstract style. He would paint ten of them in all; in the 1905 landscape, rocks and trees are depicted by geometric shapes and blocks of paint, thus foreshadowing the Cubist style. At the same time, Cézanne expresses his own fascination with the mountain which emerges as an almost mythical presence in this series of paintings—yet another trait of abstract style of painting. Cézanne's stylistic innovations like the juxtaposition of warm and cool colours as well as overlapping of forms were quite radical at the time. Yet another example of his bold experimentation appears in The Large Bathers in which Cézanne draws on the Western convention of the female nude but reimagines it in a highly individualized way. Traditional elements like the arch is replaced by the frame of trees and instead of a naturalistic depiction of the female form, the figures are painted as a conglomeration of shapes and limbs without any distinguishing or indeed recognizable facial features.

Death and Legacy

Though by the beginning of twentieth century, Cézanne's works were getting some recognition—both from critics and buyers—he had personally become more distant and unapproachable than before. Living apart from his wife and children, Cézanne spent more and more time alone, either shut up in his studio or on his own out in the countryside. In October 1906, he caught a chill from working in the fields which worsened quickly. He died of pneumonia on 22 October that year and was buried in his beloved Aix-de-Provence.

Though Cézanne was painting at the height of the Impressionist movement and even shared a few of its traits, he soon developed a highly unique artistic idiom and vision. Eschewing the temporality and effects of light prioritized by the Impressionists, Cézanne searched for greater substance and structural unity in his art. This again prevented his compositions from sinking into pure abstractions—so that even when his shapes and colours express the essence or feeling of an experience or being, they remain grounded in the real and solid. Not surprisingly, Cézanne's unique fusion of realism and abstractionism influenced soon go on to influence future styles like Fauvism, Expressionism and especially Cubism with Picasso calling him, '...the father of us all'.

Trivia

- In Emile Zola's novel *L'Oeuvre*, the character of the tragic artist Claude Lantier was reportedly based on Cézanne—which angered the latter and led to an estrangement between the two.
- In 2011, Cézanne's The Card Players sold for more than US$ 250 million, the highest price ever paid for a painting at the time. The State of Qatar was the buyer.

9. Abanindranath Tagore

The decorative details on the pillars evoke the miniature style of Mughal art though the pathos in depiction of the dying emperor is new. There is a limited colour palette as opposed to the jewel-like colours of traditional miniature painting. The figures are composed in a way that the viewer's gaze is drawn to the glowing Taj Mahal in the far-right corner—all these are the evidence of a highly individual use of the concept of perspective in Western art. All these are the distinguishing aspects of The Passing of Shah Jahan, which made its creator Abanindranath Tagore the figurehead of the Revivalist movement in Indian art at the turn of the twentieth century. His art was not just a significant aspect of the wider Bengal Renaissance that used literature, music, art, sciences and commerce to usher in social and cultural reforms but also emerged as a contributor to growing Indian nationalism of the early twentieth century.

Early Life

Born on 7 May 1871 into the culturally conscious Tagore family, Abanindranath was fortunate to be exposed to artistic influences right from his childhood. Both his older brother, Gaganendranath and their grandfather, Girindranath, were artists. His father Gunendranath along with famous poet Rabindranath were among the earliest students of the Industrial Art Society—a private initiative started by a handful of European and Indian gentlemen in 1854.

Not all European influences were benevolent. When young Abanindranath was severely flogged by the British master of the Normal School in Kolkata, Gunendranath took his son away. Soon after, the family moved to a sprawling estate in Champadani in the suburbs of Kolkata, located on the Ganges River. Here, young Abanindranath would wander around the estate park frequented by birds like peacocks, cranes, wild ducks and even animals. The mansion itself had many shuttered rooms with antique carpets, vases, paintings and other objects of art. All this fired young Abanindranath's imagination and he went about using his father's paints and brushes to put these images on paper.

Early Art

After Gunendranath Tagore died, his wife took the kids and returned to Kolkata. Abanindranath's interrupted schooling was resumed—this time at Sanskrit College. After five years there, he expressed his desire to study English and Western Sciences at St. Xavier's College. One thing led to another and in 1897, Abanindranath joined the Government Arts College to study art under European teachers like Signior Ghilardi and Charles Palmer. At college, Tagore received training in the Western artistic conventions of perspective, objective materialism, figurative style as well as the medium of oil and pastels, and painted many portraits in the last years of the nineteenth century. Two pastel-portraits Rabindranath (circa 1892), Debendranath (circa 1893), and two other paintings done years later—a sensitive double portrait of the artist's grandsons in late 1920s as well as another portrait of Rabindranath (circa 1930)—reveal the influence of early Italian Renaissance artistic style.

Growing Individualism

In 1900, a short visit to the town of Monghyr in the state of Bihar, marked another change in Tagore's artistic philosophy. Sitting on the Kashtaharini and Bisram Ghats, watching the stately Ganga flow by and reflected in natural rhythms of village life, Tagore felt dissatisfied with the subjects and themes of Western artistic conventions. Upon his return to the Tagore family home at Jorasanko, Kolkata, he stumbled upon an ancient Persian manuscript with elegant illustrations and calligraphy. Tagore's yearnings now found a medium and he began to find out more about the Indian tradition of miniature painting, of which the Mughal, Pahari and Rajput were the most important styles.

Fortunately, in 1897, Tagore had already met E.B. Havell, the new superintendent of the Government School of Art in Calcutta who openly encouraged students to learn more about the Indian miniature painting style. Though Tagore never formally became Havell's student, he began seeking out the Englishman's support and advice in his search for a new artistic idiom.

Tagore's earliest work under the influence of ancient miniature style was the Krishna-Lila series painted from 1901 to 1903, which even had Persian style calligraphy though in Bengali script! Over time his handling of the style matured and Tagore brought the pathos of human condition and suffering to the tableau-like, non-emotional style of miniature painting, seen most clearly in his famous The Passing of Shah Jahan. Completed in 1900, this painting is oil on wood and hence, shows some technical influence of his early European art training.

In this phase, Tagore was deeply interested in themes tied to the history and mythology of the land, evident from Buddha and Sujata (1901), Banished Yaksha (1904), Summer from Kalidasa's Ritu Sanghar (1905), Moonlight Music Party (1906), The Feast of Lamps (1907), Kacha and Devajani (1908), Shah Jahan Dreaming of Taj (1909), Aurangzeb Examining the Head of Dara (1911) as well as Asoka's Queen painted in 1910 for Queen Mary of England. At the same time, Tagore felt the pull of day-to-day scenes of the Indian countryside, from its villages and towns, its people and creatures. Some of the most sensitive of such paintings were The Call of the Flute (1910), Veena Player (1911), as well as a series on animals and birds of which perhaps the most touching is that of a tired camel, titled Journey's End.

Oriental Influence

To a large extent, this interest in the everyday life of people and the land was the result of Tagore's encounter with the Japanese master Okakura Kakuzo who advocated a pan-Asian aesthetic philosophy. Okakura sent two of his disciples, Yokoyama Taikan and Hishida Shunsō, to Jorasanko. From them, Tagore learnt the Japanese wash as well as ink and brush techniques and began using them to impart a dreamlike quality to his paintings especially landscapes like Dewali Shahjadpur Landscape and Ullapur Station. Among the figures in this technique belongs Khayyam series (circa 1907-09), Sun Worshipper as well as the iconic Bharat Mata painted in 1905. Coincidentally, this was the time when Lord Curzon announced the Partition of Bengal and the painting soon became the symbol of purity and spiritual strength of the country, opposed to the violence and greed of the colonial government.

Tagore's love of Mughal subjects as well its miniature style was seen in illustrations of Omar Khayyam's Rubaiyat as well as in graceful paintings of the Kashmir series like Chashma Shahi, Nasim Bagh and the poignant Night at the Shalimar: The Emperor Shah Jahan. The drama of Mughal history was also depicted in paintings like Alamgir and Aurangzeb examining the head of Dara. Indeed, Tagore would give a free play to his narrative style in the Arabian Night series of 1928-30. In these paintings, the action of the stories is vividly portrayed even as Tagore plays with the setting and subjects—sometimes including scenes and figures likelier to be found in cosmopolitan Kolkata rather than the faraway Arabian desert. In fact, art critics have interpreted Tagore's Arabian Night paintings as a rejection of the white man's Orientalist fantasy and attempt to reclaim agency for the colonized subject.

Tagore's penchant for storytelling found other expressions as well. He not only wrote stories for children but illustrated them with his own drawings. Even today, his stories 'Raj Kahini', 'Sakuntala', 'Kshirer Putul', 'Bhutapatri', 'Nalaka', 'Nahush', and 'Buro Angla' form an important part of Bengali literature for children. His sketches, postcard paintings to students, and lithographs make up the rest of his artistic oeuvre. Abanindranath's innate love for drama led him to design sets for many a play staged at the Tagore household in Jorasanko. He also wrote extensively on the philosophy and practice of art to be found in *Bharat Silpa*, *Six Limbs of Painting* and *Artistic Anatomy* as well as regular contributions to the *Journal of Indian Society of Oriental Art*.

Later Career

Towards the end of his life, Tagore evinced an interest in folk and popular art of Bengal, especially in a sub-genre known as *katum kutum*. Literally meaning twig-family, this form of art took branches, tree roots, and driftwood, fashioning out of them objects of art and mini-sculptures. This form of mixed artwork, especially from discarded material, anticipated the awareness of environmental conservation many decades before recycling became trendy. Tagore's bent towards the popular also found expression in writing *jatra* or folk plays as well as sculpting masks based on recognizable personalities.

Death and Legacy

On 5 December 1951, Abanindranath Tagore passed away, having witnessed the birth of free India. His successful search for an artistic style that was Indian in style, sensibility and themes was crucial to instilling cultural pride among Indians during the nationalist struggle. The iconic 'Bharat Mata' became the face of the nationalist movement in the realm of fine arts. At the same time, he was opposed to slavish copying of the past and cautioned his students, 'Whether you take after Ajanta or Greek or Japanese or China, it is nothing but taking to another man's way. Why should I port my boat at an alien coast when each one of us has our own?'

Tagore's artistic career can be seen as the search for his own 'way', an individual artistic idiom that was rooted in his country's landscapes, people and traditions, and yet open to new ways of looking and expressing, making Tagore the first to modernize Indian art. In the process, he popularized a distinct style that came to be known as the Bengal School of Art which eventually went on to be associated with great names like Nandalal Bose and Jamini Roy.

With his death, Tagore's descendants bequeathed most of his paintings to the Rabindra Bharathi Society Trust. The outcome has not been entirely fortunate since many of his paintings continue to gather dust in the Trust's locked boxes and cupboards—and worse, are in danger of being permanently damaged. This, according to eminent art historians, has unfortunately prevented a full-fledged appreciation of Tagore's art which could be far richer and wider than the world has known till now.

Trivia

▶ According to art historian Mukul Dey, Abandindranath Tagore was a consummate actor excelling especially in comic parts, often written for him by his illustrious cousin, the Nobel Laureate Rabindranath Tagore.

10. Vincent Van Gogh

The canvas is a playground of vibrant colours, which at the same time, exudes a harmony of effect; the brushwork is assertive and the compositions simple but evoke a sensitive appreciation of an inherent beauty. Though Vincent Van Gogh's career as a painter was short and his reputation when he was living limited, today he is recognized as a brilliant painter of the Post-Expressionism style whose influence on modern art has been immense.

Early Life

Vincent Van Gogh was born on 30 March 1853 at a Dutch town, Zundert. His father was a minister of the church and the head of a devout Protestant family that included three girls and three boys, including Vincent. Among his siblings, he was especially close to his younger brother,

Theo, seeking his advice on important matters, and was supported by him during his artistic beginnings.

Vincent received an erratic schooling starting with the village school in Zundert for a year, then going to a boarding school in Zevenbergen for two years, followed by eighteen months at a high school in Tilburg. At sixteen, Vincent was apprenticed to his uncle who owned a branch of Goupil & Cie, a Paris-based art dealership. This was young Vincent's first exposure to the world of art and involved travel to centres of contemporary artistic innovation like Paris and London. However, Vincent was soon tired of all this and his mind turned to religion. After a brief unsuccessful stint as a teacher, he decided that, like his father, he wanted to become a man of the cloth.

Though he did not complete his ecclesiastical training, Van Gogh decided to become an evangelist at the Borinage coal-mining region, in southern Belgium. His flock consisted primarily of miners and their families whose stark living conditions left a deep impact on Van Gogh. Here, he made a few sketches and watercolour drawings mainly using a Realist style. A persistent restlessness brought him back to his parents' home and after a lot of soul-searching, he decided to take Theo's advice of becoming an artist. However, his parents were no longer willing to pay for his education and Vincent now depended on Theo for both financial and emotional support. Though Vincent enrolled in art academy at Brussels, he left just after nine months and went to live with his parents at Etenne in North Brabant in April 1881.

The Early Phase

It was here that Van Gogh started practising art earnestly — initially restricting himself to pen and pencil drawing so that he could be skilled in the technical aspects of art like perspective, anatomy, and physiognomy. His palette was restricted to colours like black and white and as a result depth was achieved by play of light and shade rather than colour. The peasant life of the region usually formed his subjects, some in profile and some in static poses. His landscapes were an attempt to master perspective. Eventually, Van Gogh began a study of Anton Mauve, a master in The Hague School of Art which led Van Gogh to experiment with more colours and different media like oils and watercolours. Among the well-known paintings of this phase are Still Life With Cabbage and Clogs, and a landscape titled, View of the Sea at Scheveningen. The latter shows the beginning of Impressionist influence on Van Gogh with its short brushstrokes depicting the choppy waves and figures in the foreground, indistinct but in motion.

He then travelled to The Hague and then to Drenthe in search of newer locales and models. At The Hague, he received his first commission to paint cityscapes. More importantly, his style showed traces of a bolder use of colour and light anticipating the Expressionist style of his later years.

The Middle Phase

After an unwise romantic liaison, Van Gogh found himself once again moving with his parents at Nuenen, near Eindhoven. Influenced by the compositions of the French painter Jean François Millet, Van Gogh too began recording the lives of the peasants in his paintings, especially figures of hard-working farmers, labourers and weavers. From 1884, he began a study of heads and hands of these weather-beaten figures which turned out to be a preparation for his April 1885 masterpiece titled The Potato Eaters. Today, this is regarded as Van Gogh's finest work in his Dutch style, marked by Rembrandt-like traits of shadowy background contrasted to objects in the foreground lit with a warm glow and subjects detailed with personality and dignity.

However, soon, Van Gogh decided to formally study art once again and enrolled in the academy at Antwerp. He was unable to sustain this and in early 1886, decided to move to Paris with Theo who was by now well-entrenched in the art business of the city. Theo introduced Vincent to the contemporary artistic scene in Paris which was then enjoying the vivid works of Impressionists like Claude Monet, Paul Cézanne, Edouard Manet and post-impressionists like Paul Gauguin. Van Gogh gave up any remnants of the shadowy Dutch style and began brightening up his canvas with vibrant colours and bolder brushstrokes. Other influences from this time included George Seurat's pointillist technique that Van Gogh used in a self-portrait, as well as the craft of Japanese woodcut prints known as ukiyo-e. Living and working in the thick of so many artistic and cultural currents enriched Van Gogh's vision and style in many ways, helping him to find his own artistic idiom. By 1888, his work revealed a surety of style and confidence and he personally felt ready to move out of Paris.

The Last Phase

The destination that Van Gogh now chose was Arles in Provence where he rented a sunny villa that would also find its way in one of his paintings titled, The Yellow House. The balmy climate and the scenery bursting with flowers, fruits and fields inspired in him new heights of creativity. In spring, the reds and pinks of the orchards, and in summer, the yellow of the ripened wheat set his canvas ablaze with colour. For seascapes, he went to nearby Saintes-Marie-de-la-Mer while for portraits, members of the Roulin family posed for Van Gogh. The Sunflower series epitomizes his finest artistic abilities from this time. Though he began the series when still at Theo's house in Paris, in Arles he expanded the oeuvre, becoming increasingly daring in his colour effects, pushing the boundaries of the yellow spectrum and more evocative in details. Each painting in the series shows the flowers in different compositions and in every painting, the flower appears in a bunch, each is different in detail.

Van Gogh's creative arc appeared to rise even higher with the much-anticipated visit of his artist friend from Paris, Paul Gaugin. Both friends painted in creative fury and Cafe Terrace at Night is an instance of new artistic heights. But soon, there was a fall out. This emotional storm coupled with the delusionary effects of epilepsy that he was suffering from brought about a psychotic episode in Van Gogh. Gaguin left for Paris and Van Gogh got himself admitted to an asylum at Saint-Remy-de-Provence. His mental deterioration was rapid but on the days that he felt better, Van Gogh still painted. The hospital, as well as the surrounding grounds, olive groves and cypress trees, became the subjects he captured in a diverse range of styles. Eventually, it would be paintings of this last tortured few months that would provide the climax to a long and sometimes difficult graph of artistic growth.

Among the paintings of this time, the most famous perhaps is the 1889 oil painting titled, Irises, which depicts the flowers in brilliant hues of blue, mauve and purple while also showing the influence of Japanese woodcut prints. This, together with a previous masterpiece, Starry Night over the Rhone, was chosen to be exhibited in the prestigious annual Societe des Artistes Independant exhibit in Paris. The paintings garnered warm praise from art lovers and critics alike and finally gave Van Gogh a taste of much-deserved success.

In his last few days, Van Gogh came up with one astonishing work after the other. Wheatfield with Crows and Thatched Cottages at Cordeville are among the greatest paintings of those days. Towards the end of his life, he moved closer to the green and blue spectrum that he used with characteristic vividity and energy. At the same time, he appeared to be giving up the glimmering effects of Impressionism in favour of a conscious breaking of familiar shapes. This, along with the adoption of undulating lines to indicate movement and energy, showed that Van Gogh was moving even beyond Post-Impressionism to anticipate Expressionism and Fauvism.

Death and Legacy

Van Gogh checked himself out of the Remy asylum in May 1890 and after a brief visit to Theo in Paris arrived at the rustic environs of Auvers-sur-Oisein to paint. But his illness was at an advanced stage—on 27 July 1890, he shot himself in the chest, dying two days later.

Van Gogh's personal crises have popularized the image of the tortured genius who pours his angst onto his canvas but finds fame when it is too late. Though much behind the myth is true, the artist in him was far bigger than the myth. Van Gogh painted some of the most exquisite works in the Impressionist style and then moved beyond light-dappled landscapes to a bolder play of colours and stronger brushstrokes which mark his masterpieces in the Post-Impressionist style. Through Van Gogh, viewers saw flowers, fields and seas glowing in vivid colours as well as figures charged with emotional subjectivity. Eventually, this drama of style was further intensified, leading to distortion of shapes, intense colours and agitated strokes. Through this, Van Gogh paved the way for the more guttural style of later movements like Fauvism and Expressionism.

Trivia

- There are many versions about Van Gogh's injury to his ear. The conventional account has it that in a fit of passion after a fight with Gaugin, Van Gogh attacked his friend with a razor. In horror and remorse at his action, Van Gogh then cut off a part of his own ear. According to a later version put forward by two German historians, it was Gauguin who injured Van Gogh's earlobe while they were fencing and the story of the self-mutilation was concocted between the two to avoid arrest.
- But what happened afterwards is even more bizarre — Van Gogh allegedly packaged up the lopped off ear and gave it to a prostitute in a nearby brothel.
- To save costs, Van Gogh often painted over his artworks instead of buying new canvas.
- During his lifetime, Van Gogh managed to sell only one painting — The Red Vineyard — for 400 francs, a few months before his death in 1890. Just to put this in perspective, his most expensive painting Portrait of Dr Gachet was sold for US$ 148.6 million a century later in 1990.

11. Georges Seurat

The first impression is of a softly flickering surface but upon looking closely, one sees the figures on the canvas composed of small strokes and dots of contrasting or complementary colours. The technique came to be known as Pointillism, developed by French artist Georges Seurat. His method was underlined by contemporary scientific investigation into the realm of physics of light and colour, just as his subjects were influenced by Impressionist themes of urban leisure and modern life. Towards the end of his brief life, however, Seurat moved away from his earlier stately, dignified almost classicist compositions to a more eccentric and dynamic style, strongly influenced by pop cultural artefacts like posters and caricatures, thus anticipating future movements like Surrealism and Pop Art.

Early Life

Born on 2 December 1859 in Paris into comfortable upper-middle class circumstances, Georges Seurat was raised by his mother, while his father, a retired bailiff, lived in a cottage home in the suburbs of Le Raincy. Among the earliest artistic influences on young George was his mother's family which had several sculptors. During his training at the École des Beaux-Arts, he came across contemporary quasi-scientific theories about the mutual impact of lights, lines, colours, geometry and music on the final work of art in books such as *Essay on the Unmistakable Signs of Art*, by Humbert de Superville, and another by David Sutter. Later, he met Michel-Eugène Chevreul—a 100-year-old chemist who had propounded the theory of the chromatic circle of light—and also read Ogden N. Rood's *Modern Chromatics* (1879). All this led to Seurat becoming interested in the scientific basis of art throughout his life.

Early Phase

This was also the heyday of Impressionism which often featured scenes of urban and middle-class pursuits. In keeping with this convention, Seurat got busy in mid-1880s with painting scenes from the popular picnicking areas like Asniers and the island of Grand Jatte. The result was his first masterpiece, Bathers at Asnières, completed in 1884 but which the state-sponsored Salon refused to put up in its exhibition. Seurat and several other artists then founded the Société des Artistes Indépendants, where he finally exhibited Bathers in June of 1884. His next two years were spent to complete a mural-sized painting titled A Sunday on La Grande Jatte, which is considered his best artwork from this phase. This was followed by another painting in the same style, Grandcamp, Evening 1885, and the following year, La Grande Jatte was exhibited in the eighth and last Impressionist Exhibition.

Artistic Innovations

Though the influence of Impressionism was clear in the subject and use of vivid colours, it was evident that Seurat was using a technique of his own. Instead of focusing on how the subject appeared in a particular kind of light, Seurat adopted a more detailed approach. But what caught the particular interest of Impressionists like Signac and Pissarro as well as the art world of Paris was Seurat's new technique of Pointillism which involved juxtaposing small dots or strokes — points — of different colours. The final effect was that of a blending of colours not on the canvas, but optically in the viewer's eye. This was a completely new way of using colours in art which till now had been mixed on the canvas by the artist or available as pre-blended pigments.

The other technique that Seurat would go on to develop was the related one of Divisionism based on his theory that separating colours into individual dots or patches would lead to the greatest luminosity scientifically possible. The effect of these techniques on Seurat's paintings was indeed a higher vividity of colour and a gentle flickering, evident in a later composition, again based on Grand Jatte, titled La Seine a la Grande-Jatte (1888).

Later Phase

Seurat's moving away from Impressionist themes became more apparent from the 1890s. Young Woman Powdering Herself, completed in 1890, featured his mistress Madeleine Knobloch — but instead of the calm, stately figures of his earlier works, this hints at the frivolity of the action. Besides, the open window in the background and objects at the dressing table indicate a deepening interest in the upcoming style of Symbolism. These growing influences are clearer in the painting titled Circus Sideshow (1887-88) where geometric patterns like circles and rectangles in the background led to varied symbolic interpretations by critics. Seurat was now clearly more interested in popular entertainment like circus and fairs, to which he would return in his last masterpiece. Titled Circus, this was finished in 1891 and depicts a scene of greater motion and action than he ever painted. The growing influence of contemporary popular art forms like posters is also evident in this painting. According to art historians, this painting was based on an 1888 poster printed for the Nouveau Cirque of Paris. The painting remained incomplete as Seurat died suddenly of infectious angina on the Easter Sunday of 1891.

Legacy

Apart from his seven masterpieces, Seurat also made forty smaller paintings, and around 500 drawings besides filling several books with sketches of landscapes and figures. Though he took off from Impressionist concerns with appearance of light and colour as well as depiction of modern urban life, Seurat went much further with artistic innovations and wider subject matter. The development of Pointillism and Divisionism in his search for greater vividness of colours as well as including more popular recreational pursuits in his themes led influential Félix Fénéon, art critic of the times, to coin the term 'Neo-Impressionism'—a style that Seurat embodied in his works of art.

Seurat's later paintings also reveal his deepening interest in the way certain shapes and objects can be used to express certain moods, emotions and meanings—the essence of Symbolism, that would sweep the world of arts and culture in the early twentieth century.

Trivia

- Though Seurat hid his mistress's identity from even his closest friends and family, he officially acknowledged his son—evident in the entry of the child's name in the register of births as Pierre-Georges Seurat.
- The child died within two weeks of Seurat's death from the same infection and was buried alongside Seurat at the Père-Lachaise cemetery in Paris.
- 'Great things are done by a series of small things brought together'—this quote by Seurat best exemplifies his techniques of Pointillism and Divisionism.

12. *Frida Kahlo*

The vibrant colours and intense brooding of the self-portrait are evidence of an artistic genius pressed down by emotional and physical pain, yet determined to make them visible on canvas. The style is deeply symbolic, where objects and recurring motifs stand for deeply personal as well as community experiences. Frida Kahlo, not surprisingly then, was the forerunner of art articulating gender and postcolonial consciousness in a time when such theories were yet to gain global currency.

Early Life

Frida Kahlo was born on 6 July 1907 in Coyocoan, Mexico City, into a multiracial family. Her father was German while her mother had Amerindian and Spanish heritage. This mixed racial ancestry would later impact her art in the form of questions about her own identity as well as stylistic elements. Frida grew up in the family's home which was known as the Blue House or Casa Azul, deriving the name from its cobalt-coloured walls. This would also be where she would return to live and work till her death in 1947.

Despite contracting polio in her childhood, Frida was encouraged by her father to lead an active life, swimming and even wrestling and playing cocker—sports which were rather unusual for girls in those times. In 1922, Frida joined National Preparatory School in Mexico City and quickly became part of an anti-establishment group of writers and artists. Among them was the budding painter Alejandro Gómez Arias with whom Frida became romantically involved. On a September afternoon, the two went out, but the bus they were on met with a serious accident. Frida was severely injured—her spine and pelvis were fractured while her hip was impaled with a steel handrail. For several weeks, she remained in the Red Cross Hospital in Mexico City and even when she was finally allowed to return home, she had to be in a full body cast for three months.

It was during this time of recovery that Kahlo started painting. Her parents encouraged the new interest seeing that it kept their daughter's mind off her pain and loneliness. They bought her paints and canvas, and ordered a special easel so that she could paint in bed.

Self-Portraits

Inevitably, the first few paintings were self-portraits. As Frida would later say about her penchant for painting her own self—'I paint myself because I am often alone and I am the subject I know best'. As many as fifty-five out of 143 paintings were self-portraits done at various stages of her life.

During her convalescence, a mirror had been placed above her head so that she could see her own reflection from the bed where she lay and draw self-portraits. At this time, she was more influenced by the realism of her father's photography art and hence her self-portraits such as Self-Portrait in a Velvet Dress in 1926 and Self-Portrait: Time Flies as well as portraits of her sisters and school friends are made in the representative style though imbued with acute psychological intensity. The brush with mortality had left her with questions about the meaning of her life, her purpose on earth and a feeling of dissociation.

Later, her self-portraits expressed the anguish of her emotional life, especially as she fell in love with famous Mexican artist Diego Rivera and got married, not once but twice. All this would go into her self-portraits, the best of which were Portrait of a Woman in White, Self-Portrait Dedicated to Leon Trotsky, Self-Portrait With Cropped Hair and Two Fridas in which she is depicted separately in native Tehuana colours as well as in European dress—

marking two different personas that were attracted and then betrayed by Rivera. Self-Portrait With Monkey (1938) and Self-Portrait With Braid (1941) are other self-portraits from the later period of her life.

Pain

'My painting carries with it the message of pain.' Right from her childhood, physical conditions like polio drove her awareness of the body and its attendant vulnerabilities. However, her accident in 1925 had the biggest impact on her painting, expressing feelings like physical pain and anguish at her immobility to emotions like sadness and loneliness. The Broken Column drives home the horrors of her injury and treatment in unsparing detail—her skin is riddled with nails, her body is in a surgical brace since it is split in the middle with the spine exposed like a dilapidated but decorative column. In all, Frida was subjected to thirty-three surgeries and the pain inflicted by medical treatment itself was depicted in a painting in 1945, Without Hope, which shows the horrific experience of forced feeding. Towards the end of her life, Frida again suffered from a gangrenous foot and had to undergo repeated surgeries. The Wounded Deer was painted in 1946 and from this time she continued to identify herself with the wounded mythology of St. Sebastian.

Womanhood

An important theme of Frida's paintings was the physical and emotional stress associated with birth and miscarriage like Frida and the Miscarriage as well as My Birth. Frida suffered repeated miscarriages which not only left her physically traumatized but also anguished about the inability to bear children. At the same time, these paintings explore different meanings of fertility—not just as the power to bear children but to create art, contribute to politics and love other creatures.

In many of Kahlo's self-portraits, she is accompanied by monkeys, dogs, and parrots, all of which were her pets. Critics have interpreted them variously. According to some, they have mythological or religious connotations—monkeys signify lust and dogs are creatures of the underworld. Other critics have seen them as surrogate figures for the children that Frida could not bear—this is especially borne out by the pet's collar drawn as a red ribbon which could also represent the umbilical cord, thus indicating how the artist, who could not bear children, became mother to all Creation. Eventually, these paintings became more than thematically important as Frida's growing artistry with symbols led to her emergence as a foremost Symbolist and even Surrealist painter.

Yet another aspect of the womanhood explored in Frida's paintings relates to her marriage with Rivera. In

Frieda and Diego Rivera, she sees herself as a dutiful wife in a Mexican dress, holding her husband's hand, while Rivera holds the tools of a painter—as though in her role of a wife, Frida needed to give up her identity as a painter herself. The 1937 painting, Memory, the Heart, expresses Kahlo's pain over Rivera's affair with her younger sister, Christina. Eventually, she also explored the conventional markers of womanhood, especially related to hair, drawing a series of self-portraits with braided hair, cropped hair, curly hair and loose hair—as though asking who determines what it is to be a woman and how she could contest those notions.

Mexican Identity

Even before marrying Riviera, Frida was conscious of her Mexican identity. Various self-portraits like Time Flies and Self-Portrait depict her wearing the vibrant coloured clothes, shawls and accessories from the Tehuana region of Mexico. Equally importantly, she adapted certain artistic techniques from previous Mexican painters such as the use of a background of tied-back drapes in self-portraits and *retablo*—an indigenous style depicted through small traditional devotional paintings with Catholic iconography—evident in My Birth and My Grandparents, My Parents, and I (1936). Eventually, she would be remembered as one of Mexico's most important painters.

Death and Legacy

After struggling with ill health, Frida Kahlo succumbed to a pulmonary embolism in 1951. She is remembered as one of the foremost women painters of the world who made female self-expression an instrument of art. Works like What the Water Gave Me and especially later ones like Wounded Deer and Weeping Coconuts were in the style of high Symbolism, even anticipating Surrealism in their depiction of a fantasy world of dreams, pain and death. However, Frida herself was ambiguous about any labels. When famous Surrealist painter, Andrew Breton, described her paintings as Surrealist, she responded, 'I never paint dreams or nightmares. I paint my own reality.'

Trivia

- The bus accident in her youth fractured Kahlo's right leg in eleven places.
- For her only solo painting exhibition in Mexico City, she arrived in an ambulance.
- Casa Azul was home to many of Kahlo's pets which included a Mexican hairless breed of dog called Xoloitzcuintli, an Amazon parrot named Bonito, a fawn called Granizo, an eagle with the impossible nickname of Gertrudis Caca Blanca, and two spider monkeys named Caimito de Guayabal and Fulang Chang, the last of which had its own titled painting.

13. Amrita Sher-Gil

The vivid colours and bold strokes are reflected with an unhesitating directness in oil on canvas. The theme is an unusually frank glimpse into an intimate moment of women's lives—the decking up of a prospective bride. However, the figures appear pensive and even sad. This emotional realism is contrasted with touches of figurative style that seems to look beyond representation. The Bride's Toilette is now one of the masterpieces of Amrita Sher-Gil, the Indian-Hungarian artist who, in her brief life, energized the Indian art scene and set it squarely on the path to modernism with her signature blend of Indian and European elements.

Early Life and Art

Born on 30 January 1913 in Budapest to a Hungarian mother and Indian father, Amrita Sher-Gil had a cosmopolitan upbringing, often straddling two continents, countries and their cultures. Her uncle, Ervin Baktay, an Indologist and a painter, was one of the earliest experts to recognize young Amrita's talent for painting. With his encouragement and supported by her father's resources, Amrita enrolled at the École des Beaux-Arts in Paris when she was only sixteen. Here, she absorbed the best that the city had to offer which was then enlivened by the Post-Impressionists and nascent Expressionists. Amrita was particularly influenced by artists such as Paul Cézanne, Amedeo Modigliani and Paul Gauguin. The works from her Parisian phase includes self-portraits, city scenes, nude studies, still lifes as well as portraits of friends and fellow students. In her brushstrokes, figures and light, there is the distinct influence of Post-Impressionists. For example, her Self Portrait as Tahitian has echoes of French post-Impressionist Paul Gauguin's dark-skinned Tahitian female subjects. However, in the oil titled Young Girls (1932), the colours are jewel-like and the subjects—one of them being her own sister, Indira—are often non-European. The painting won gold medal and Sher-Gil was elected as an associate of the Grand Salon in Paris in 1933. At twenty, she was the youngest ever member and the only Asian to become an associate. Sleep, completed in 1933, is a nude portrait, again of Indira, powerful in its confident brushstrokes as well as its sensuality.

Return to India

Soon, however, Sher-Gil became restless and in 1934, decided to return to India. The change in landscape, light and the very air led to the realization that her future as an artist lay not in blind copying of European conventions—no matter how avant-garde—but in depicting the people and places of this sun-baked earth. While in Saraya, Sher-Gil would write to a friend, 'I can only paint in India. Europe belongs to Picasso, Matisse, Braque.... India belongs only to me.' To know India and her artistic traditions better, she set off for a trip to the southern part of the country. On the way, she came upon the wall paintings of Ajanta in Maharashtra. This was a moment of revelation to the young artist and she was greatly impressed by the rich hues, the elegant figures as well as its narrative style.

Growing Assurance

At that time, the Indian art scene was dominated by the Bengal School, led by Abanindranath Tagore. He had drawn liberally from India's miniature art tradition, particularly the Mughal style, besides mining the country's rich mythology and history for subject. At the same time, he had been strongly influenced by the simplicity and wash techniques of Japanese art. Tagore's style had been perpetuated by his most famous students like Nandalal

Bose, Jamini Roy and Abdur Rehman Chughtai and this had resulted in the predominance of the Bengal School marked by water colours, sparse landscapes, graceful strokes and a tendency to create binaries between the objective materialism of the West and the spiritualism of the Orient.

Sher-Gil rejected such hard, artificial distinctions and found Indian art of the 1930s dull, bleak and lifeless. At the same time, she was aware that the alternative was not an en masse import of Western artistic conventions. In her search for a new style to express the Indian subjects and sensibility, she found the wall paintings of Ajanta and the sculptures of Ellora a rich source of inspiration. Though in her graceful lines and elongated shapes, her style continued to reveal influence of the Bengal School, Sher-Gil's canvas, in contrast, began glowing with the reds, ochres, yellows and greens while there was a new visual reality in her figuration. The results of her travels across southern India were three major paintings titled, Bride's Toilet, Brahmacharis, and South Indian Villagers Going to Market. Apart from the distinctively new style, these paintings reveal a new attitude to the subjects — rather than being patronizing and sentimental, these recognize the hard life of the Indian common people but with empathy. These paintings are also significant for viewing women through a different lens — neither eulogizing, nor pitying their condition but understanding their concerns and challenge to live a life of dignity amidst many hardships.

After her travels, Sher-Gil returned to Hungary where she recalled her European conventions to paint works like Hungarian Church Steeple, Nude, Potato Peelers, Winter and Hungarian Peasant. In 1938, she married her cousin Victor Egan after which the couple then came back to India to stay at the paternal ancestral estate in Saraya in Uttar Pradesh. Here, she began painting women from the village as well as the servants who would come over to work at her father's home. Village Scene, In the Ladies' Enclosure and Siesta are the major works from this time. The colours are vivid as before but the shapes appear to have become more angular indicating the daily hardships of life for the common labouring classes. The figures are often huddled together and look in different directions. While these still depict sombre expressions, the mood is not merely one of suffering but often invoking the leisurely rhythms of life in rural India. Animals increasingly form the subject in paintings such as Elephant Promenade, Bathing Elephants and Camels (1941), one of her last completed paintings which reveals her growing desire to use form and lines to convey the abstract that lies at the heart of realism.

In 1941, Sher-Gil and her husband moved to Lahore, which was then a thriving cosmopolitan hub of the arts. Right before her first solo exhibition, Sher-Gil collapsed and slipped into a coma. She died on 5 December 1941 — she was only twenty-eight. The last works of Sher-Gil, most unfinished, reveal a definite shift from representation towards greater abstraction even as they come alive with a palette of more diverse colours than anything she had painted before. Her artworks from this last phase like Woman at Bath (1940) show a more expressive representation of the female figure—her works were the first to anticipate modernist trends in India.

Personal Life

Throughout her brief life, Amrita Sher-Gil lived as passionately as she painted. In Paris, she was known as a vivacious young woman, with many friends and lovers, well on her way to career in the fine arts. However, listening to her heart, she returned to India in search of a new artistic idiom. At Shimla, she became close to British journalist Malcolm Muggeridge who recognized her 'enormous joy in the sensuality of the world, in things growing, in animals, in colour—which was what gave her painting its tremendous vitality'. Indeed Sher-Gil once described herself as 'sensualist of the eyes'.

However, this innate sensuality gave Sher-Gil's parents, despite their cosmopolitan outlook, many sleepless nights and they are believed to have burnt many of Amrita's letters, possibly some written to future Prime Minster of India, Jawaharlal Nehru.

Sher-Gil was also thought to enjoy a strong bond

with the painter Marie Louise Chassany, and some art critics such as artist Vivan Sundaram, her nephew and biographer, consider the painting Two Women a reflection of their relationship. However, in a 1934 letter to her mother, she insisted that she and Marie Louise were never involved with each other 'in sexual terms.'

In 1938, Sher-Gil surprised many, including her parents by deciding to marry her Hungarian cousin, Viktor Egan, who hardly had any material prospects. The marriage may have been caused by Sher-Gil's hope that Egan would be able to help end her unplanned pregnancy. In the end, it could have been another botched abortion that led to Sher-Gil's death.

Death and Legacy

After Sher-Gil's death, most of her paintings were handed to National Gallery of Modern Art (NGMA), New Delhi. Today NGMA has as many as 107 of her paintings, covering the entire spectrum of her artistic career, from her Parisian works to her Indian paintings.

'Fundamentally Indian' was how Amrita Sher-Gil came to describe her own artistic style. Using oils in the manner of her French training, she nevertheless considered it her artistic mission 'to interpret the life of Indians and particularly of the poor Indians pictorially, to paint those silent images of infinite submission and patience, to depict their angular brown bodies'. Even more significantly, Sher-Gil was the first Indian woman and indeed one of the earliest women painters in the world to go beyond the conventional depiction of the female form as an object of male gaze. Instead, she infused it with agency and natural expressions which in Indian subjects would range from melancholia and resignation to serenity.

Trivia

- Sher-Gil's Sikh father, Umrao Singh Sher-Gil was an aristocratic estate owner with a passion for photography. Many of his photographs document the childhood of two sisters, Amrita and Indira.
- As a child, Amrita was expelled from her convent school in Shimla for declaring herself an atheist.
- The day after her death, Britain declared war on Hungary and Viktor was sent to jail as a national enemy.

14. Pablo Picasso

The colour palette is limited, simple geometric shapes meet the eye and the overall impression is that of a painting made up of blocks viewed from different angles. This is what you can expect in Cubism, a style most associated with Picasso. The prolific painter is regarded as one of the giants of the history of world art who also invented collage, influenced Surrealism and created sculptures and prints, besides designing for the stage and ceramic works of art.

Early Life

Born on 25 October 1881 in Malaga, Spain, to an art professor named José Ruiz Blasco, Pablo was experimenting with lines and colours as early as age ten. Realizing his son's potential, Blasco began training the budding artist and helping him with models and resources.

In 1895, the older artist was offered the post of an art professor at the La Lotja, Barcelona, where the whole family moved in the autumn of the same year. Young Pablo was enrolled in the same academy to fulfil his family's expectations as much as his own ambitions. For the same reason, two years later, he set off for Madrid to study art at the Royal Academy of San Fernando. But eventually, he became more interested in recording day-to-day life around him as seen in the cafes, streets, brothels and markets.

Madrid also acquainted young Pablo with the best Spanish art history. Here, he got to know Velasquez and Goya and was deeply influenced by their use of subjects from Spanish culture like bullfighters and Celestina, who would appear in Picasso's own paintings in different times over his career. Due to an illness, Pablo had to move to the Catalan countryside to recuperate. The change of scenery helped the budding artist to gain clarity about other matters too—he decided to depart from his art school training and forge his own artistic style. Equally significantly, he now started using his mother's surname to sign his works—Picasso.

Even after returning to Barcelona and acquiring notice as an artist with promise, Picasso remained restless. In 1900, along with his studio mate Carles Casagemas, he decided to head for Paris where his work had already been selected for the Spanish section of the Exposition Universelle. In the art capital of the world, Picasso expressed the bright colours of fashion, young models as well as the buzz associated with the World Fair through his use of charcoal, pastels, watercolours and oils.

The Blue Period (1901–1904)

However, this effervescent phase was not to last. A turbulent love affair lead to the violent death of Casagemas and Picasso was left shaken by the experience. From this brush with tragedy emerged his paintings of the Blue Period of 1901, including two death portraits of Casagemas, two funeral scenes titled Mourners and Evocation as well as the mystery-laden La Vie. These works were marked by shades of blue to depict abject figures like old blind men, street beggars and women prisoners.

The Rose Period (1904–1906)

Once Picasso decided to shift permanently to Paris, his art seemed to brighten up as evident from the paintings of so-called Rose Period like Family of Saltimbanques, The Actor and Girl on a Ball. He was now looking to explore new stylistic influences as well as subject matters like the travelling circus, street performers and acrobats. It was as though these performers, always on the move, reflected the flux in the lives of modern artists such as himself. The use of earth and flesh tones in this period was more pronounced in paintings The Harem, Two Nudes, La Toilette as well as his Portrait of Gertrude Stein and a Self-Portrait with Palette in which Picasso seems to be increasingly interested in sculptural forms.

The natural culmination of Picasso's growing confidence in exploring styles and themes was seen in a work of great impact titled Les Demoiselles d'Avignon (1907). This depicted women from the brothels of the eponymous Barcelona street that was popular with sailors. The depiction of such women without traditional filters of tenderness and pathos and with the full acknowledgement of their naked power was itself a break from previous artistic norms. Appropriately, such a ground breaking theme was accompanied by stylistic innovations like use of striations, African masks in place of heads and the fracturing of the subject's faces.

Another significant influence in Picasso's work from this time was that of Cézanne, especially as transmitted by a new friend Georges Braque. This is evident in subjects like still lifes as well use of shallow space and planar brushwork, typical of the Frenchman's paintings.

Cubism

Picasso had long been moving away from the perspective and representative styles that dominated artistic convention since Renaissance. Now, he was ready to adopt a new style that depicted figures and landscape almost as geometrical shapes in palettes of ochres, browns and greys. This is clear in his works from 1909 to 1912 such as Factory at Horta de Ebro, Ambroise Vollard, Daniel-Henry Kahnweiler and a series of seated figures sometimes playing musical instruments such as those in The Accordionist. This style came to be known as Cubism which seemed to aim at showing figures from multiple axes, points of view and even light sources, thus often portraying both ears and eyes, nose, lips etc. of the same face on the canvas. This was again in keeping with the dominant intellectual trends of the time, according to which, reality is not unitary, objective or a matter of straight unbroken perspective. Instead, the same event or figure can be viewed from different perspectives, giving different results, all of which are real.

Soon, Picasso had moved even further from Cubism to a more assimilative notion of art. Thus, began his so-called 'Synthetic phase', starting with creation of collage which involved gluing of paper and other material like sand and wallpaper onto the canvas. This style used more colour and took for its themes, still lifes and masked heads of the previous stages. Eventually, Picasso's works began to synthesize more with more varied elements. For instance, Glass of Absinthe is part collage and part sculpture and painting; unlike the subject depicted, the artwork itself is clearly two-dimensional. At times, the elements in his work seemed to transform into one another—for instance, the bend of a guitar could seem like the curve of an ear in some of the paintings from the Guitar series.

First World War

With the onset of the First World War, Picasso found himself drawn into an avant-garde circle of artists who frequented the Café de la Rotonde in Paris. His friendship with the French poet Jean Cocteau led Picasso to design the set and costumes for *Parade*, a ballet that included modern iconography like skyscrapers, airplanes and typewriters. In keeping with the instinct for artistic rebellion, Picasso's set laid open the clash between elements of realism like the stage curtain and fantasy expressed by the cubist design of the stage props and costumes.

Return to Barcelona in 1917 led to a distinct phase in Picasso's art which has been labelled 'New Mediterraneanism'. This was marked by classical bent, both in theme and style seen in paintings like portrait drawings of Max Jacob and Ambroise Vollard as well as in Three Musicians. At the same time, he kept designing for the stage which brought him both fame and money.

Surrealism

The horrors of one world war and the clouds of another turned the thoughts of artists towards the realm of fantasy where shapes, lines and colour took on dreamlike manifestations in the form of grotesque figures and troubled emotions. This led to a movement known as Surrealism and Picasso was influenced: Paintings such as Crucifixion and Minotaur are infused with Surrealist imagery. However, it was through words that Picasso was able to give more definitive expression to his surrealist imagination. For around a year, he practically gave up painting and instead wrote poetry which was published as collections titled *Cahiers d'Art* (1935) and *La Gaceta de Arte* (1936). In 1941, he also wrote a Surrealist play titled *Le Désir attrapé par la queue or Desire Caught by the Tail*.

Politics and Art

Political events have always had an impact on artists and Picasso was no different. In 1935, the country of his birth was torn apart by the Spanish Civil War. In 1937, Picasso produced a series of etchings and aquatints titled Dream and Lie of Franco. However, his most famous work on Spain was Guernica, a mural painting commissioned by the Republican government to put up at the Spanish pavilion of the World's Fair that was being hosted by Paris in 1937. The artwork was named after the Basque town bombed by the Fascists in the same year. Hence, it depicts the horrors of war, its imagery of the fallen soldier, the wounded horse as well as anguished mothers with their dead children. The expression of violence in both form and gestures continued with his skull-like drawings as well as depiction of the claustrophobic atmosphere during the war years. Occasionally though he would produce paintings of intense colour like the Weeping Woman and Still Life with Red Bull's Head.

With the end of the Second World War, Picasso joined fellow Parisians to celebrate the liberation of the city. He threw his paintings of the past five years open to public view but the reaction was one of discomfort. This intensified even further when he decided to join the Communist Party. But Picasso had already moved on to other things—a new mistress named Francoise Gilot, a new locale of the Antibes and a new medium too, ceramics. The most famous paintings of this time were Joie de Vivre which reflects his ecstasy in love as well as nymph-like portraits of Gilot. This showed a return to classical traditions in the treatment of mythological creatures. Many of his Mediterranean phase paintings depict young children in various actions and poses—owing as much to the experience of fathering his own kids with Gilot as to a greater artistic fecundity and virtuosity.

At the same time, Picasso was compelled by a stronger identification with his Mediterranean origins, evident in his ceramic artwork in which plates, jugs, and vases, obtained from the Madoura potters were painted, reshaped or marked by fingerprints and even scratched by Picasso. He continued to lend his artistic touch to many political causes — designing the dove of World Peace Congress poster in Wrocław, Poland as well as painting two panels titled War and Peace for the Temple of Peace in Vallauris.

Later Years and Death

The last phase of Picasso's life and work was inspired by a new muse, Jacqueline Roque, whom he married in 1961. Towards the end of his life, he became increasingly interested in history of European art and began creating variations of famous paintings by famous artists of the past such as Édouard Manet, Rembrandt, Eugène Delacroix, Gustave Courbet, and especially, Velázquez. This was a clear attempt to include himself in the tradition of the Old Masters. Likewise, artworks of his final days can be thought of as looking back on his own artistic trajectory. His vast paper cut-outs and acting in movies such as *Le Mystère Picasso* (1956) marked a return to the figure of the harlequin and circus performer.

On 8 April 1973 at his hilltop villa in Mougins, France, Picasso died of a heart attack and was interred at the Château of Vauvenargues near Aix-en-Provence.

Legacy

Picasso was a truly prolific artist. He left behind a staggering body of work in a career spanning roughly eight decades—13,500 paintings, 100,000 prints and engravings as well as a stupendous 34,000 illustrations for books. He also produced 300 sculptures and ceramic pieces and even in his last days, continued to create and experiment with various media, forms and colours. As he was well-paid for his art in his early days, he was able to keep for himself around 50,000 works in various media from every period of his career. From this collection, a sizeable selection was passed onto the French state while the rest was inherited by his heirs.

Today, Picasso is best known for his association with movements such as Cubism and Surrealism that opened entirely new ways of viewing the world and its experiences. In the play of more vivid colours and intense gestures, his last works anticipate Neo-Expressionism of the mid to late 1970s.

Trivia

- Picasso finished his first major 'academic' painting when he was only fifteen years old. It is titled First Communion and is a portrait of his parents and younger sister kneeling before an altar.
- Picasso died in the middle of a dinner he and his wife were hosting for visitors.
- Thirteen years later, his widow Jacqueline Roque shot and killed herself—she was fifty-nine years old.

15. Georgia O'Keeffe

At times the close-up startles with its compelling details while at other times, the shapes and colours push everything else into the background. Intense naturalism of the flowers has such effect that it seems to symbolize something more. This power of abstraction in the natural world of landscape, flowers and foliage is what Georgia O'Keeffe is famous for. This also led her to be hailed as the first American Modernist painter who would go on to influence later icons of the style, such as Arthur Dove and Aaron Douglas. Equally important was her success as a woman painter since she charted a difficult path between biologically essentialist readings of her paintings and life on her own terms.

Early Life

Born on 15 November 1887, near Sun Prairie, Wisconsin,

Georgia O'Keeffe was fortunate to grow up in a family which recognized and nurtured her artistic talents. She received the same encouragement from her school, and upon graduating high school, she left Wisconsin to study art. From 1905 to 1906, O'Keeffe attended the Art Institute of Chicago and the Art Students League in New York City. Though trained in the imitative realist style that was the convention of all formal art education at the time, O'Keeffe aspired for a more personal, experimental idiom.

In the summer of 1912, O'Keeffe attended an artists' workshop conducted by Alon Bement of Teachers College, Columbia University, in New York City, who in turn introduced her to the modernist thinking of Arthur Wellesley Dow. He was one of the first American proponents of the idea that rather than representing objects exactly as they were in nature, artists should use them to convey their own ideas and feelings. Dow also favoured the Japanese philosophy of *notan* which was about the arrangement of lighted and darkened parts of an artwork.

Early Art

Inspired by Dow's ideas, O'Keeffe began teaching art at Columbia College in southern California. But soon she was venturing further in her search for an intensely personal artistic language. The result is seen in her earliest masterpieces No. 3—Special and Blue No. 2 painted in

1915–16 in which the lines and colours appear to convey certain emotions of the artist. Towards the end of 1916, she moved to Texas to join the Arts Department at the West Texas State Normal College. The endless plains and wide horizons of the state as well as the spectacular physical features of the canyons aroused her artistic instinct in dramatic ways leading to compositions like watercolours, such as Sunrise and Little Clouds II (1916), Evening Star nos. II and VII (1917), as well as Light Coming on the Plains (1917). Mostly painted in water colours, these artworks depict O'Keeffe's tendency to draw from nature, deeply personal ways of artistic expression.

In 1916, O'Keeffe had already met and received encouragement for her artistic endeavours from famed photographer Alfred Steiglitz. In 1918, she moved to New York City and the two started living together, even though Steiglitz was a married man and older to her by twenty-four years. They would finally get married in 1924 after Stieglitz managed to get a divorce. In the meantime, he offered to support O'Keeffe's artistic efforts for a year.

Middle Phase

For a while, O'Keefe continued with her abstractionism such as Red and Orange Streak / Streak (1919) but she was increasingly showing an inclination to draw large scale close-ups of flowers and other recognizable natural forms as seen in Petunia No. 2 (1924) and Black Iris (1926). Possibly influenced by the art of photography, these depicted the magnified forms of floral still life and intricate details. Some critics of the time interpreted the detailed depiction of the flower's reproductive features as metaphors for female sexuality but O'Keeffe rejected such essentialist notions. Instead of any implicit or explicit symbols, she merely wanted to express the essence of a flower, though on a magnified scale. About her themes and style, she said, 'Nobody really sees a flower—really—it is so small—we haven't time—and to see takes time... So I said to myself—I'll paint what I see—what the flower is to me but I'll paint it big and they will be surprised into taking time to look at it.' The other famous painting from this time is the Radiator Building (1927), which again depicts the play of lines and shapes—in contrast to the tall, straight lines of the building are the diffuse, curved shapes of smoke rising upward. The play of light as from the electric illumination and dark as in the night sky backdrop is another artistic highlight of the painting.

New Mexico

From the 1930s, O'Keeffe began growing apart from Steiglitz as well as the New York City art hub. She visited New Mexico a few times and was captivated by the starkness of the desert landscape and symbols. This found its way into her painting and the most famous example is the Cow Skull of 1931. The sharp edges and weathering of the skull are depicted with amazing precision, showing a continuation of her hyper-representative style of the flower series. At the same time, the skull taken out of the desert landscape and given the background of blue, red and while colours could convey concerns ranging from oppressive nationalism to environmental degradation or most likely the reality of death.

In the summer of 1933, personal and professional stress caused a nervous breakdown, to recover from which, O'Keeffe moved to Bermuda for some time. Eventually, she returned to New Mexico and purchased a ranch which would be her home for the rest of her life. Paintings like From the White Place (1940), Pelvis IV (1944), Black Place III (1944), Black Place, Grey and Pink (1949) are clearly inspired by the traditional architecture as well as the open, desert landscape around her—largely bleak and monotonous and hence, all the more striking when broken by reds and pinks—indicating her emotional attachment to the place. Such has been the influence of these themes in her paintings that today, they are sometimes identified as 'O'Keeffe country'.

Later Phase

From 1960s, O'Keeffe again returned to an abstract style,

painting a series of water, land and sky compositions often from unusual perspectives like from the window of aircrafts. Examples of such work are Blue, Black and Grey (1960) and Sky Above Clouds IV (1965). These were characterized by massive scale, high horizon and often simplified shapes of clouds all of which convey human wonder at the vastness of sky and space.

From 1970s, her failing eyesight led O'Keeffe to experiment with other media like clay, pastel and charcoal. In this, she was encouraged and assisted by sculptor, Juan Hamilton. The two also worked together on a book titled *Georgia O'Keeffe* (1976), as well as a film, *Georgia O'Keeffe* (1977). Worsening health compelled O'Keeffe to move to Santa Fe, where she died two years later, on 6 March 1986.

Legacy

Georgia O'Keeffe is regarded as one of foremost American Modernist painters. Her use of abstractions to express her own emotions and ideas was pathbreaking in the America of the 1910s and '20s. At the same time, she insisted her paintings were more than means to convey symbols, especially the essentialist kind which focused on her gender and sexuality. Instead, her contribution to feminist art was more substantial — she was among the first woman painters in the world to make a living from the sales of her art. Even more incredibly, she continued to own almost half of her total works, and as a result, at the time of her death, her estate was worth more than US$ 70 million!

Trivia

- To paint under the New Mexico desert sun, O'Keeffe often converted the backseat of her Model-A Ford car into a studio.
- Well into her 70s, O'Keeffe still went camping, and at 74, she even went on a rafting trip.
- In 1946, O'Keeffe became the first woman to earn a retrospective at the highly prestigious Museum of Modern Art, in New York City.
- Her favourite landscape in New Mexico was a table mountain called Cerro Pedernal visible from the front door of her New Mexico home, Ghost Ranch.

16. *Edvard Munch*

The skeletal face twists in agony, mouth and eyes agape in horror as the curved lines clash in an unnamed experience of intense anguish—though paintings are inaudible, this one titled Scream is deafening in its depiction of the tortured human psyche. An icon of modern art, it was painted by Norwegian artist Edvard Munch, whose paintings are famous for the portrayal of psychological conditions such as depression, fear and anxiety in the Symbolist style. This style moves beyond the realistic representation of objects to depict them as a compound of powerful symbols and personal significance. Eventually, he became one of the pioneers of the Expressionist style, experimenting with graphic art and films.

Early Life

Born in 1863 at a rustic farmhouse near Loten, Norway, to a military physician father, Edvard Munch ironically grew up amid illnesses and insanity. One of the most traumatic experiences of his childhood was his mother's death from tuberculosis—he was merely five. No sooner than he found a surrogate maternal figure in his older sister Sophie, she was taken away by the same disease. To add to young Edvard's misery, his father, Christian Munch became mentally unstable, developing an intense religious fanaticism that interpreted the family's illnesses as punishment of divine origin. During the rare times he would be well, he would narrate stories of supernatural terror, often by Edgar Allan Poe, to his young children. Surrounding the family always would be a sense of impermanence and abjectness as because of Christian's work, the family moved frequently and lived in relative poverty.

As a child, Munch himself would remain sick most of the time—partly because of the family's vulnerability to tuberculosis and partly owing to the long, harsh Northern winters. Not being able to attend school and forced to remain indoors, young Edvard took up drawing and painting initially as a way of passing time.

Soon though, young Munch would show signs of artistic genius—especially a bent towards unconventionality. This would be further strengthened by his friendship with Hans Jæger who was at the heart of a bohemian, anti-bourgeois group that advocated, among other things, sexual freedom and the abolition of marriage. Under Jæger's influence, Munch began drawing more from personal experience; the result was works such as The Sick Child (1885-1886) depicting Sophie in her illness as well as a fine lithographic Self-portrait (1895), in which his head and clerical neckband materialize out of a dark background underlined by a skeletal hand. Indeed, Munch would go on to write in his private journal that 'I inherited two of mankind's most frightful enemies—the heritage of consumption and insanity—illness and madness and death were the black angels that stood at my cradle.'

To compound the complexity, Munch felt desperately in love with a married society lady named Millie Thurlow. Ecstatic and agonized in equal measure, Munch would go on to express the end of the romantic liaison in later paintings, especially in his Frieze series.

Despite all the emotional tumult in his life, Munch attracted enough notice as a budding artist to get a state fellowship to go to Paris in 1884 for studying art under Leon Bonnat. The same year, his painting Morning was accepted for display in the Norwegian pavilion of the Exposition Universelle hosted in Paris.

Mature Phase

In Paris, Munch was exposed to the Impressionist style of painting that was a rage — the delicate play of light and shade as well as the glimmer of colours seemed a far cry from his own darker themes and denser treatment. Personal loss continued to inspire his art as evident from Night in St. Cloud (1890) — a melancholy depiction of an empty room marked by a shadowy cross that he composed after receiving news of his father's death.

Next followed a period of frequent travel between Paris and Berlin since Munch received a commission to paint for a frieze in the German capital. At the heart of this work was a series of six love-themed paintings, the earliest of which dated to 1893. These were collectively titled 'Frieze of Life - A Poem about Life, Love, and Death' (1893) and harked back to the intensity of his affair with Millie. After being displayed in the Berlin Secession in 1902, the paintings brought Munch much-deserved fame in contemporary cultural circles and improved his family's financial condition as well. Artistically, the Frieze paintings are a proof of his maturing style which now found expression in innovative brushstrokes including scraping and rubbing, bolder colours besides his trademark haunted feeling. Many art historians also include in the Frieze group, other masterpieces by Munch from this time like Melancholy, Jealousy, Despair, Anxiety, Death in the Sickroom and The Scream, which he painted in 1893. Later works such as Madonna, Puberty and Self-portrait with Cigarette, painted in between 1894 and 1895, are evident of a more experimental style but continue his persistent concern with themes like illness, despair and death. Towards the end of the decade, Munch also became interested in photography, though he never explored the artistic possibilities of the medium at par with painting or printmaking.

Later Phase

A life continuously lived on the edge of artistic and emotional intensity brought about a nervous breakdown in 1908 and Munch had to be hospitalized in Copenhagen. Upon his release next year, he left for Norway to avoid the temptations of a dissolute lifestyle. There, he took refuge in Ekely, an 11-acre estate that he bought on the outskirts of Oslo. The change is reflected in his paintings, both thematically as well as stylistically. The fresh Scandinavian landscape now featured as his subject besides the farming life and labour of the countryside. Likewise, his art now made use of lighter colours and looser brushstrokes to convey a more optimistic feeling. Among the greatest works from this period are The Sun (1910-1911), Spring Ploughing (1916), and Bathing Man (1918). Now and then though, Munch would return to life long concerns of death and mortality as evidently from a series of self-portraits that he did during the 1930s and '40s. Finally, after struggling with deteriorating physical condition, caused both by degenerative eye disease as well as by the nervous strain of wartime bombings, Munch died in his country home on 23 January 1944.

Legacy

For a man who had willed all these works of art — including 1,008 paintings, 4,443 drawings and 15,391 prints, besides a treasure trove of woodcuts, etchings, lithographs, copperplates and photographs — to the government of Oslo, he is ironically remembered by a single painting, The Scream, partly because it is considered an iconic work of modern art and partly because of its reputation as one of most expensive paintings: It was sold for more than US$ 119 million at Sotheby's in New York in May 2012. Nevertheless, Munch was an artist whose Symbolist style gave visual expression to the early twentieth-century concern with the human psyche, its depths and despairs. In moving beyond representative art, he heralded the abstract idiom of German Expressionism and even Surrealism — thus being enshrined forever as one of figureheads of twentieth-century visual art.

Trivia

- Only one of Munch's early nudes, Standing Nude, have survived—the others are believed to have been destroyed by his religious fanatic father.
- Nazi dictator, Adolf Hitler, called Munch's paintings 'degenerative art' and ordered them to be taken down from the walls of German museum. Ironically, his funeral was hosted by the same Nazi regime which used it as propaganda to gain favour in Norway.
- The psychological intensity of Munch's art is evident from his description of the setting that would later be recreated in The Scream. Out walking with two friends at sunset, he suddenly felt like the 'air turned to blood' and the 'faces of my comrades became a garish yellow-white' and subsuming it all, was the sensation of 'a huge endless scream course through nature.'

17. *Salvador Dalí*

The images crawl out of the canvas like nightmarish tendrils from some half-feared, half-forgotten dream. The lines depict familiar objects but in bizarre shapes and hallucinatory settings. This is how Dalí reinterpreted the world and art as projection of the desires and urges of the unconsciousness—all familiar hunting ground of Surrealism. Eventually, Dalí would go on to develop a distinct technique known as 'paranoid critical' defined as a hyper-imaginative condition in which one could mimic the state of being in a delusion while still being grounded in sanity. By mid-twentieth century, this technique would be widely applied beyond visual media, starting with cinema to literature and even fashion.

Early Life and Work

Born Salvador Domingo Felipe Jacinto Dalí i Domènech on

11 May 1904 in Figueres, Spain, the future art sensation grew up in comfortable middle-class environs. Both his lawyer father and homemaker mother encouraged young Salvador's early forays in art. As he grew up in the Catalan town, he internalized its flat, often rocky landscape which would feature repeatedly in his later art. By the time he was in his late teens, young Dalí was already experimenting with Impressionist and Pointillist styles at the Madrid School of Fine Arts, and at nineteen, he even had his own solo exhibition of paintings.

Young Dalí, however, would come into his own as an artist as the result of two major influences. The first was famous Viennese psychoanalyst Sigmund Freud's theories about the power of the unconscious part of the psyche on human behaviour and personality. Dalí now began exploring ways to represent the workings of the unconscious and to do this, the second source of influence came in handy. After being dismissed in 1926 from Special Painting, Sculpture and Engraving School of San Fernando in Madrid for insulting a professor, Dalí left for Paris. He visited fellow Spaniard Picasso at the latter's studio and the event turned his life around. Dalí now became aware of the latest artistic theories and techniques like Cubism and Symbolism as well as the nascent forms of Expressionism and Surrealism. In the abstract forms and deep subjectivism of these styles, he found the artistic idiom to express his own feverish artistic imagination. Apparatus and Hand

(1927) is the best work of this early phase in which he used the symbolic imagery and dreamlike landscape that would come to characterize his unique artistic style. In fact, he even extended this style to films, collaborating with avant-garde director Luis Buñuel on two films, *Un Chien Andalou* (*An Andalusian Dog*, 1929) and *L'Age d'or* (*The Golden Age*, 1930). Later, Dalí would lend his art to the dream sequences of *Spellbound*, a 1945 film by Alfred Hitchcock, starring Gregory Peck and Ingrid Bergman.

Middle Phase

Dalí's films caught the attention of the Surrealists in Paris and Andre Breton invited him into their group. Dalí was now launched into the most innovative artistic periods of his career and the results are evident in a series of iconic paintings in the Surrealist style of which the most famous is perhaps the Persistence of Memories (1931). Against the flat dreary landscape, the painting depicts unrelated and bizarre objects such as melting clocks and scurrying ants. The painting has been interpreted in various ways — standing for the decay wrought by passing time or even the Postmodernist notion that it was no longer possible to understand time as definite and linear — rather, it is non-rigid and indefinite. The Great Masturbator, the Enigma of William Tell, Soft Construction with Boiled Beans were other important works of this time when Dalí was keen on giving expression to timeless human fears and obsessions, especially those related to sex, death, violence and memory. The threat of dominance by the female or father figure were direct echoes of his Freudian preoccupations, which, in turn, were often visualized through grotesque, explicit human forms, nevertheless depicted with an exacting technical artistry.

These years were also an emotionally turbulent time for Dalí. Through the Parisian Surrealists, he had been introduced to Elena Dmitrievna Diakonova, wife of Surrealist writer Paul Éluard. The two came together in a physical and emotional attraction that rocked even the largely permissive Parisian high art circles. Nicknamed Gala, Diakonova not only became Dalí's muse and lover, but soon his business manager, and after divorcing Eluard in 1934, his wife as well.

Dalí's emotional tangles had already constrained relations with some Surrealists. This was further complicated by his ambiguous position regarding Fascism and Communism, depicted in paintings like the Enigma of William Tell and Premonition of Civil War as well as in his portraits of Hitler.

In the 1940s and '50s, Dalí began experimenting with other media as well — objects like Lobster Telephone, Mae West sofas as well as a whole range of jewellery designed in his inimitable wacky style.

In America

Dalí left with Gala for North American shores during World War II and was met with media frenzy upon his arrival. In 1941, The Metropolitan Museum of Modern Art in New York gave him his own retrospective exhibit. The very next year, Dalí's autobiography was published under the title *The Secret Life of Salvador Dalí* (1942). All these were ways he built up a larger-than-life public persona including wearing outlandish clothes and accessories.

The physical separation from European mainland also ushered in stylistic changes in Dalí's art. He now began working in a more classical context, evident in paintings such as Galarina, The Poetry of America, Tristan and Isolde, The Temptation of St Anthony and The Madonna of Port Lligat. Eventually, the complex religious and classical themes were fused with contemporary theories of science and mathematics, especially nuclear physics in the aftermath of the nuclear explosions and dropping of the nuclear bomb in 1945. Dalí himself described this period as the phase of 'Nuclear Mysticism.' Paintings of this time were usually spread across huge dimensions but expressed through fine details that were both technically brilliant in imagination and phantasmagoric as seen in Young Virgin Auto-Sodomized by the Horns of Her Own Chastity. Very often, his religious themes like in Crucifixion (Corpus Hypercubus) (1954) would jostle with geometrical concepts such as the tesseract as a way of exploring the fourth dimension. Increasingly, he would incorporate holography and optical illusions in his art work like In Voluptas Mors (1951) which appears to be a skull from a distance but on closer inspection turns out to be composed of female nude forms.

Later Art and Death

After his return from America to Figueres, Dalí got busy with rejuvenating the cultural scene of his hometown. He undertook the building of Teatro-Museo Dalí (Dalí Theatre-Museum) in Figueres which finally opened to the public in 1974. Though built on the ruins of an old municipal building, the Theatre-Museum was designed by Dalí himself as a complex of spaces in which each element is part of another—the building is today considered the largest Surrealist structure in the world.

Dalí went through a period of financial uncertainty due to botched up business relations. However, with the support of wealthy patrons, Dalí was saved from ruin. Still, misfortune continued to dog him—a neurological condition forced him to retire from painting in 1980, his beloved Gala died in 1982, and in 1984, Dalí himself was burnt severely in a fire at his isolated castle-like home at Pubol. Towards the end of his life, he returned to his city of birth where on 23 January 1989, his heart finally gave way at the age of eighty-four.

Though the Surrealist movement in art and culture did not originate with Salvador Dalí, today he is remembered as its most famous and powerful artist. Even though he was later criticized for crass commercialism, obsession with TV appearances and letting his antics overshadow his creativity, his best artwork continues to be valued for plumbing the depths of the human unconscious. They reveal disturbing, erotic, violent and fantastic forces that lie hidden, just beyond the veil of the everyday, familiar reality.

Trivia

- Dalí was as much famous for his surrealist art as his persona of the provocateur — he wore exaggeratedly long moustache and a cape besides carrying a walking stick.
- In 1934, at a New York exhibition ball held in his honour, Dalí made a characteristically flamboyant entry — wearing, across his chest, a glass case with a female undergarment.
- Dalí appeared in advertisements for chocolate, Scotch and Alka Seltzer.
- Dalí once created a shaving foam painting live on TV for the show, *I've Got a Secret*.

18. *Andy Warhol*

Screen-printed images in neon colours sit side by side with abstract, even impersonal tone of the canvas. Subjects range from iconic sex-sirens to soup cans to self-portraits—but that is how Andy Warhol saw the world. Anything or anybody could be the focus of artistic interpretation and in the process, he redefined high art to include popular images, styles and diverse media. Warhol, as the pioneer of Pop Art, thus not only erased the strict boundaries between gallery and commercial art but reinvented the persona of the visual artist as flamboyant, highly successful and the man of the masses.

Early Life and Work

Born on 6 August 1928 into an immigrant Czech family as Andrew Warhola, Warhol grew up in a house of limited means. However, his mother, a deeply religious Catholic lady, was also fond of art and would encourage young Andy to fill his colouring book. Another reason Andy became interested in art was because in the elementary school, he contracted chorea, also known as St. Vitus' Dance. The disease affects the nervous system of the patient leading to involuntary spasm and movements. As a result, young Andy was forced to stay at home for several months, during which he drew and painted to pass time.

Growing up with an unusual complexion, Andy was painfully shy and preferred to keep to himself and his artwork. At the same time, he was also fascinated by movies, and in his young days, started a collection of photos autographed by his favourite movie stars. Many of these would later find their way in his artwork.

After high school, Warhol enrolled in the Carnegie Institute of Technology, where he graduated in 1949 with a major in pictorial design. During his college years, he discovered the blotting line technique in art. This entailed taping two pieces of blank paper, drawing with ink on one and quickly blotting it on the other. The blotted image would have irregular and lightly smudged lines which would then be filled with water colours. Even after college, Warhol used this technique for commercial art projects like I. Miller shoes, Tiffany & Company Christmas cards, besides illustrating Amy Vanderbilt's *Complete Book of Etiquette* as well as book and album covers.

Middle Phase

However, the blotted line technique was tedious and very time-consuming. So, Warhol turned to paint and canvas but choosing the theme turned out to pose greater difficulty. By the mid-1950s, Expressionism in art had run its course—art had become excessively abstract and personal to be able to connect with viewers. In England, this was giving way to more realistic representations of recognizable objects, most of which belonged to the realm of daily use.

On the other side of the Atlantic, Warhol too was taken by this popular style art and began hand painting Coca Cola bottles on full-size canvases (1962). In conscious rejection, this series is marked by bland white background devoid of any symbols. Just the Coca Cola bottle in black stands as a solid figure demanding attention.

Late Phase

Warhol's fascination with everyday objects would move into another realm with the Campbell's Soup and Brillo boxes series of mid-1960s. In this, he drew from his profession as an ad designer as well as the technique of a commercial artist to come up with bold images that almost deified objects of daily use. Like soda bottles, he now visualized soup cans and scrub boxes as subjects of art. Such objects were the new obsession of an expanding consumer class in America which revelled in abundance and supermarket images. Like all great artists, Warhol not only represented the reality of the times but used the very images to create an undercurrent of irony—instead of people and ideals, objects had become the icons of this generation.

The new theme was accompanied by a new technique as well—screen-printing. With his growing popularity after the Coca Cola series, he needed a faster way to produce his artworks and screen printing provided the solution. In this, a stencil created on a silk—or a more affordable and durable material later—was applied with ink and then printed on paper or canvas. This ancient technique of Chinese origin was hardly accorded the status of art because of the use of mechanical equipment. However, in Warhol's hands, the technique acquired new vividness because of his creative and varied use of ink—the same image could be printed but in different colours and combinations.

Though this technique would be used in the Campbell Soup and Brillo Boxes series, today Warhol's silk-screen prints are most remembered for their images of Marilyn Monroe. With her death in 1962 due to an overdose of sleeping pills, the world media was awash with her images. Warhol obtained a black-and-white publicity photo of the of the sultry actress from a 1953 film *Niagara* and used it to create several series of silk screen printed images—in varying colours and permutations, the most striking one against a gold background that was titled Gold Marilyn Monroe (1962), thus showing the influence of Byzantine Christian art in which the Holy Virgin or Child was often painted in a similar gold background.

In all, Warhol's artwork was fed by the media frenzy resulting from Monroe's death but was also an ironic comment on the commercialization of cultural icons—no matter how rare the talent, it was capable of being taken to the level of mass production, like the image of a soup can or cola bottle. The artwork was a comment on the insatiable consumerist culture—the population was seen as moving from consuming products to people as well.

Yet another highly influential silk screen print series was titled Death and Disaster (1963) in which graphic images of gruesome accidents, car crashes and other fatal incidents were cropped from newspapers and printed using the silk-screen technique. This was Warhol's comment on one of the ways modern humans were being desensitized to the daily horrors around them through media exposure and consumption of images—no matter how serious they were.

In the wake of President Richard Nixon's 1972 visit to China, Warhol created a series of portraits of the then powerful Chinese communist leader, Mao Zedong. Titled Mao (1972), these were made again by the silk screen printing technique and in huge dimensions—some as large as ten by fifteen feet. This was Warhol's way of representing Mao's personality cult and the way he lorded over the social, political and cultural landscape of China. At the same time, by painting several such portraits and stacking them against the wall, the subject could be interpreted as having been reduced to yet another mass-produced commodity in an ironically capitalist market.

Growing Innovation

The 1960 and 1970s were the most creative years of Warhol's career during which he used multiple media and techniques to express his art. One of these was film, especially in the durational style. Some of his films such as *Sleep*, *Empire* and *Eat* would go on to become iconic studies in experimental film techniques and continue to be studied in film institutes across the world. In his career Warhol made over 650 films across a wide spectrum of themes ranging from life in the recognizable settings to gay culture and experiences.

In the '80s, Warhol continued to push the boundaries of artistic expression, though his work in the '60s became more popular as representative of the Pop Art movement. In his latter phase, Warhol would dabble with abstractionism as in Rorschach based on the famous psychological tests which — like abstract paintings themselves — represented a projection of the viewer's thoughts as well as Oxidation

Painting (1976) made by—believe it or not—urinating on a horizontally placed canvas of copper paint, then leaving it to oxidize, resulting in patterns of brilliant shade and depth.

Towards the end of his life, Warhol began collaborating with younger artists like the Italian Francesco Clemente and Haitian-American painter Jean-Michel Basquiat. With the latter, Warhol produced General Electric with Waiter (1984) to which he lent his trademark advertising logos, while Basquiat brought in elements of upcoming graffiti art. Last Supper and Self-Portrait are final attempts at exploring larger than life themes; indeed, by placing himself in his gallery of portraits of iconic figures, Warhol seems to be painting himself in the tradition of great artists and their subjects.

Death and Legacy

On 22 February 1987, Warhol developed complications a day after undergoing a routine gall bladder surgery, and died at the age of fifty-eight. Today, he is acknowledged as a pioneering figure of the Pop Art movement in America and for popularizing it across the world. His use of varied mediums, wide range of themes—from everyday objects to cultural icons as well as his own Bohemian but highly commercially successful life—made people rethink the very definition of art, how it is made, valued, appreciated — indeed, consumed — in these unabashedly materialistic times.

Trivia

- Warhol's studio was named 'The Factory'.
- On 3 July 1968, Warhol was shot by small-time actor Valerie Solanas in the chest and even declared clinically dead. However, at the hospital, the doctor cut Warhol's chest open and massaged his heart — the intervention worked and his heart started beating again.
- Part of Warhol's trademark look was black glasses and silver wig, of which he possessed several.

19. Wu Guanzhong

The ink wash drawing on the canvas belongs to traditional Oriental techniques while the stylistic elements like abstract patterns indicate Western modernist influence. It is this fusion of the two conventions that made Chinese artist Wu Guanzhong one of the most important art icons from outside Europe. Surviving the restrictions on artists during China's Cultural Revolution, he became a role model for many younger artists from the East. Wu was the first living Chinese artist to be given a solo exhibition at the British Museum in London in 1992. Since then his works have been exhibited in almost all major art centres of the world.

Early Life

Born on 5 July 1919 at Yixing in the Chinese province of Jiangsu to parents employed in the education sector, young Wu was expected to pursue a conventional career. He even enrolled in the Zhejiang Industrial School to study electrical engineering but a chance visit to an art college changed the course of his life forever. He was so impressed with the paintings he saw that he decided this was what he wanted to do for the rest of his life.

Rebelling against his father, Wu dropped out of his engineering course and left for Hangzhou to study art at the National Academy of Art, now known as China Academy of Art, from where he graduated in 1942. Five years later, aided as much by his early training in the French language as by his art skills, he was fortunate to enough to be accepted at the École Nationale Supérieure des Beaux-Arts in Paris where he studied art from 1947–50. Paris, during this period, was the hub of avant-garde art, represented by the criss-crossing of modernist styles like Neo-impressionism, Post-impressionism, Expressionism and Abstractionism. Wu too was caught up in these surging times and was most influenced by the works of Vincent van Gogh, Henri Matisse, Maurice Utrillo, Paul Gaugin and Amedeo Modigliani.

Early Art

After returning to China, Wu began teaching at the Central Academy of Fine Arts in Beijing. His willingness to teach Chinese students Western oil techniques and modernist styles like Formalism did not sit well with the Chinese political establishment. His use of these elements, as well as the subject of nudes in his own artworks, increasingly caught the ire of authorities. The Portrait of a Lady, painted in 1962, is one of the rare paintings from this time to survive. The style is European Impressionist but the features of the figure is clearly oriental. Not surprisingly, Guanzhong thought it prudent to destroy his nude artworks and little else survives from this early artistic phase.

One of the most famous paintings from this time is titled Twin Swallows in which static form of traditional Jiangnan architecture forms the background to the motion of two swallows as they fly towards a tree. In the dominance of geometric shapes, use of depth and perspective, this painting is representative of Wu's early Western influence. Despite his budding reputation, in the late 1960s Wu found himself barred from writing and teaching, and in 1970, he was sent to Hebei Province for forced, manual labour as part of nationwide crackdown on artists and intellectuals during the Cultural Revolution.

Middle Phase

It was only in the 1970s, that Guanzhong was allowed by the Chinese authorities to return to painting—initially to paint murals and decorations in hotels. With the death of Chairman Mao in 1976, artists could breathe a little more freely. By then, a definite shift had come about in Wu's artistic style and vision—to some, driven by political compulsions. He began focusing on landscape and architecture that marked the horizons of his own country. Likewise, rather than the oils of his youth, Wu began working in ink more frequently, adopting the centuries-old ink and wash techniques. Towering mountains are common Wu's landscapes from this phase. These depict not only the regal peaks of northeastern China from the many sketching tours that he took across the country but also look back at eleventh-century Chinese masters like Guo Xi and their iconic works like Early Spring.

Wu's persistence as an artist even in the face of troubles paid off and by 1978 his works were being featured in the Central Academy of Fine Arts (CAFA) in Beijing. By this time, he was experimenting increasingly with abstract elements, looking for a way to bridge the immense distance between Chinese and Western aesthetic sensibilities. His shift in style, from representation to semi-abstraction, becomes clear with the mural, titled The Great Wall, painted for Beijing's Xiangshan Hotel in early 1980s. His painting Lion Grove (1982) is a more acclaimed representative of this search for a new artistic idiom. The use of lines and dots to depict the largest rockery in Suzhou shows he had moved away from the monochromatic, long-view, representative style of traditional Chinese ink art landscapes to greater interest in how shapes, forms and colours can convey the artist's sense of a place. Another example is his Rice Paddies series, where he paints the Chinese landscape using both oils and ink, infused with planes and strokes verging on abstractionism, yet identifiably Chinese in subject.

Another way that Wu tried to synthesize traditional and modernist elements was to bring to the fore rural Chinese architecture. Instead of the natural scenery of old Chinese ink art landscapes, he now focused on the simple yet imposing structures of Chinese homes in villages and towns. The bold geometric lines and sense of weight express his renewed interest in Formalism from his early days in Paris and which now he would use as a starting point for greater abstractionism. A Quadrangular Yard (1999) is an example of this type which takes an overhead perspective and frames its subject with thick black brushstrokes. The scale is evident only because of the depiction of a tiny bird pecking at the ground. In contrast, the city view in Chongqing of the Old Times (1997) is more historical. Another work is A Big Manor from 2001 where the straight lines and geometric shapes convey the beauty of substance and form. The swathes of black and white are broken by a small red square in the foreground to induce just the right amount of colour while the monochromatic composition is given depth by the wash in the background and foreground. In contrast, the later Metropolis, dated 2005, brims with colour in geometric shapes.

Writings on Art

The play of different styles, techniques and traditions in Wu's search for an individual artistic idiom led him to write about art on many occasions. One of the most influential of his writings was *Abstraction and Form*, published in 1992, in which he described his mid-career ink phase as an attempt to use 'eastern rhythms in the absorption of western form and colour...' Later, he would use both ink and oil, seeing each as indispensable to creating a new Chinese aesthetic, indeed as 'two blades of the same pair of scissors used to cut the pattern for a whole new suit'.

Ever since Wu's return to China from France, he was concerned about the need to develop a new Chinese artistic sensibility which would remain grounded to traditional rhythms and yet incorporate the best of Western innovations in form and abstraction. This search was complicated by political censorship but rather than getting disheartened, Wu saw the barriers as challenges necessary to make his art keener, fly higher. 'Art is like a kite,' he said, 'you have to pull the string hard in order to stretch it to its limit, but you don't want to pull it so hard that you break the thread, because the thread connects you to the land and its peoples.' After the Cultural Revolution,

Wu revived his Formalist style and oil techniques so as to bring Chinese art with global directions. He proclaimed, 'To nationalize oil painting and to modernize Chinese painting: in my view these are two sides of the same face.'

About his writings, Wu later said, 'Whatever I have written is to try to help our own people to understand and to get rid of their fear and suspicion of abstraction in Western art.' Indeed, according to him, abstract beauty could be one of common areas where the East and West could meet and understand each other. Just like a child intrinsically attracted to a kaleidoscope, Wu said that the appreciation of beauty of form, colour and lines was common to people from varying cultures.

Death and Legacy

After seeing his art being recognized and appreciated not only in his own country but across the world, Wu died on 25 June 2010, at the ripe old age of ninety. He left all his art to museums in China, Hong Kong and Singapore, thus proving with his work and art more than any ideology how much he valued his connection to the people.

While he was alive, Wu rejected the Cultural Revolution notion of art as an instrument of social realism. But in his themes, he asserted the organic connection with the people, landscapes and monuments of China. At the same time, his use of colour, oil, focus on forms

WU GUANZHONG

and abstractionist approach are all evidence of his wider, international vision.

Trivia

- During the Cultural Revolution, Wu himself destroyed most of his own work—especially oil paintings—so that the Red Guards could not get to them.
- During his years of forced rural labour, there were times when Wu had to use manure bucket as an easel for his paintings.
- For thirty years, Wu kept travelling to the remotest hill regions of China to search for mountains to paint in his landscape.

20. Maqbool Fida Husain

The colours are bold swathes of red, indigo, black and yellow against which ivory figures are executed with thick angular brushstrokes. The style draws from Cubism with its non-representational style and emphasis on two-dimensional plane of the canvas but the shapes are more heavily delineated and thus reminiscent of Indian temple sculptures. The subject is quintessentially Indian—two of the country's most famous rivers, the Ganga and the Yamuna, are depicted in their mythological avatar. The river goddesses are seen in a conjoined stance, symbolizing the eternal dialectic in the self, nature and cosmos but since the dramatic moment is taken from the ancient Indian epic *Mahabharata*, it can also be thought to represent the internecine strife between the Pandava and Kaurava cousins, who were descendants of Ganga, the river goddess. This enormous diptych propelled its creator, Maqbool Fida Husain, more popular as M.F. Husain, on to the world art stage and announced the arrival of a painter of wide-ranging imagination.

Early Life and Art

Born on 17 September 1915 in Pandharpur, Maharashtra, into a Bohra Muslim family, the future painter grew up in the town of Indore in Central India. In his boyhood, he was sent to a madrasa in Baroda, Gujarat, for a traditional Islamic education. It was there he first discovered the beauty of calligraphy and recognized his own desire to pursue the fine arts. In 1931, at the age of seventeen, Husain won a gold medal for an oil painting at the Indore Art Exhibition. Three years later, two of his watercolour landscapes sold for ten rupees each which to him then seemed a princely sum as he later revealed in a 1979 interview with *India Today*, 'The sale gave me tremendous self-confidence. Even my most expensive paintings haven't given me the same thrill.'

In 1937, he arrived in Mumbai, then known as Bombay, to study art at the Sir Jamsetjee Jeejebhoy School of Art. After finishing school, he made around thirty-six paise a day by painting movie hoardings. Painting on such a large scale—since these had to cover huge billboards—Husain later reflected, was probably what led to his technique of freehand drawing, trained him in a steady hand and influenced his sweeping canvases in future. Around this time, he also designed and made toys in workshops to make a living.

His first major artwork was exhibited in 1947 by the Bombay Art Society. His art began to be noticed and in the same year Husain, along with five other painters — F.N. Souza, S.H. Raza, K.H. Ara, H.A. Gade, and S.K. Bakre founded the Progressive Artists Group. Rather than being united by a common artistic style, members of this group subscribed to a common mission of breaking Indian art free from the revivalist traditions of Bengal School and instead allowing it to take flight into 'absolute freedom of content and technique'. The independence from British colonial rule as much as the country's Partition were important influences on the avowed radicalism of the Group's style. One of his best-known works from this early phase is titled Man, painted in 1951.

Wider Influences

In 1953, Husain went to Europe for the first time where he saw the paintings of Pablo Picasso, Henri Matisse and Paul Klee by whom he was particularly influenced. These were masters of the Expressionism and Cubism and the exposure to their works brought about a definite shift in Husain's style as well. In his famous Battle of Ganga and Jamuna, Husain would include a mass of figures on the right of the canvas to symbolize the human cost of war in the manner of Picasso's iconic Guernica.

In 1955, the Lalit Kala Akademi—the highest Fine Arts Institute headed by the government of India—awarded Husain the National Award. This included a cash prize of ₹1000, then a considerable sum. During this time, his works began to sell for ₹800. The first serious collector of Husain's paintings was Badrivishal Pittie of Hyderabad.

One of the masterpieces of Husain's early phase is Between the Spider and the Lamp, painted in 1956. It depicts a row of five women with one of them holding a lamp and one spearing a spider. They are headlined by a string of indecipherable Indic hieroglyphics. The painting is alive with his signature traits like vivid colours, play of geometry, strong draughtsmanship and at the heart of it all, an unerring sense of drama.

Mature Phase

The 1970s and 80s marked a period of growing assurance and popularity for Husain as a painter. In 1971, Husain was invited to the Sau Paulo Biennale to exhibit his works along with the iconic Cubist painter Pablo Picasso. For this, he painted the earliest of his famous *Mahabharatha* series which would go on to comprises twenty-seven paintings. From this series a diptych titled, The Battle of Ganga and Jamuna would eventually be sold for a then record sum of US$ 1.6 million at Christie's South Asian

Modern and Contemporary Art Sale. In India, Husain's growing world reputation got him first major commercial order when major consumer goods brand Hindustan Lever commissioned a 60'X 48' painting.

Among the best-known works from these decades are series on mythological figures such as that of Goddess Durga. Some of these paintings were even related to contemporary politics. For example, the painting titled War Goddess Durga: Three (1981) depicts political symbols related to Prime Minister Indira Gandhi whose strong leadership proved crucial to India's win in the 1971 war with Pakistan. Then, there was the Ashtavinayaka series on the Hindu Elephant God, Ganesha.

Husain also became famous for his paintings based on historical figures such as Mahatma Gandhi, Hitler and Mother Teresa. Among natural figures, horses were a subject to which Husain kept coming back repeatedly throughout his artistic career—depicted either as free, galloping, or as still, sombre. These magnificent animals at times symbolized elemental energy and freedom while at other times, frustration, bewilderment and even like the one in Picasso's Guernica—open mouthed horror at man's cruelty against Nature and Creation.

Apart from figures, Husain painted both urban and rural landscapes like his series on Rajasthan, Benaras and *Kolkata* as well as more abstract subjects. Other famous paintings of this phase were Zameen, based on the horrors of the Bengal famine as well as Cyclonic Silence, a poignant response to the natural disaster that had affected the southeastern coastal state of Andhra Pradesh.

In keeping with his eclectic style, Husain would also repeat certain symbols and motifs in his art like an abstract hand depicted in a benedictory protective mudra. This gives evidence of his shifts from Expressionist to modernist style of painting. Apart from a multitude of themes, Husain was also experimenting with techniques. Passage Through Human Space, completed in the mid-1970s, was a series of watercolours.

Growing Popularity and Film-making

Growing fame, both critical and popular, began coming Husain's way. He was awarded all the major civilian honours of India starting from the Padma Shree in 1955 to Padma Bhushan in 1973 and finally Padma Vibhushan 1991. He was nominated as a Member of Parliament to the Rajya Sabha in 1986.

As early as 1967, Husain had made a movie titled, *Through the Eyes of a Painter*, which received the National Film Award for Best Experimental Film in India. It was set in rural Rajasthan, depicting scenes of daily living but filmed in Surrealist techniques and set to traditional Hindustani music. This was also screened at the Berlin Film Festival where it went on to win the Golden Bear

Award. Later, Husain would periodically renew his association with film-making through highly publicized initiatives. In 2000, Husain directed the movie *Gaja Gamini* as a tribute to his then muse, the Bollywood actor Madhuri Dixit. The film imagines Madhuri's character representing the many attributes of a woman's strength and beauty — as such, she is depicted as the Kalidasa's Shakuntala, da Vinci's iconic Mona Lisa, as a personification of India's musical heritage and even as a rebel. In the mid-1990s, Husain also made several paintings with the actor and her films as his subject. His next cinematic muse was another Bollywood actor Tabu around whom he would weave his *Meenaxi: Tale of Three Cities* and who would also inspire his art ventures publicized live to the media.

Political Trouble

Though Husain found himself targeted as early as mid-1990s by extremist cultural groups for insulting Hindu goddesses in his paintings, these were fringe incidents. Starting in 2006, however, Husain found himself caught in a series of protests backed by fundamentalist Hindu political parties against his irreverent depiction of Hindu goddesses. At the heart of the controversy was a red female nude figure in the shape of the Indian subcontinent made for an NGO raising funds for earthquake victims of Kashmir which titled it as Bharat Mata or Mother India. Though Husain denied naming the painting so, fundamentalist cultural organizations as well as their political patrons took offense and with the media publicizing the incident, the matter quickly snowballed into a major controversy. The Kerala government announced that Husain was to be awarded its prestigious Raja Ravi Verma Award. But the charge of insulting Hindu faith was renewed and even petitions were filed in the Kerala High Court which led to a stay on the award until the petition was disposed off.

The ripples of trouble were felt across continents. Husain's first solo show in London the same year was attacked by vandals spray-painting several of the works displayed there. Though scheduled to be open for the entire summer of 2006, the show was shut down just two weeks after its opening.

On the other side of the political spectrum, conservative Muslim organizations objected to a certain song from his film *Meenaxi*, alleging it contained words from the Holy Quran. About these incidents, he later said, 'I think you don't do work for controversy alone, and whenever you do new work which people don't understand and they say it is done to create controversy'.

Later Phase

In 2006, Husain left India and initially lived in London and then in Dubai. For the Museum of Islamic Art in Doha,

Qatar, Husain accepted a commission for ninety-nine paintings. The opening of the Museum in 2008 featured the first of the series by Husain and two years later, he accepted Qatar's offer of citizenship for which he had to give up his Indian citizenship.

The highest sum commanded by a Husain painting till date is US$ 2 million at a private sale in London that took place in October 2005. Despite many troubles with even a leading politician declaring a bounty on the artist's head, Husain never totally stopped painting his vision of his country. In 2008, he completed a highly moving piece called Rape of India, unveiled at the Serpentine Gallery in London in December 2008 in the group exhibition, 'Indian Highway.' An acrylic painting in his typical massive proportions, this artwork was made up of two disjointed canvases, depicting two cows locked up in a bloody conflict. A woman and child are caught up in the strife with the former shown dismembered by the division between the canvases. The painting can be seen as the metaphor of the surge in fanatical, violent attitudes in India which have turned on its own people—rending its inclusive fabric in two.

One of his last works was the India Civilization series, commissioned by Mrs Usha Mittal, wife of steel magnate Lakshmi Mittal, as a tribute to India's long, varied and rich history. The series was originally conceptualized as comprising of ninety-six panels out of which eight triptych works were completed. The paintings weave traditional Indian and well as religious iconography with well-known historical figures, ranging from politics and culture to common people of the country, interspersed with Husain's personal vision of India and her history. Not surprisingly, he described the ambitious project as 'a museum without walls'. Beginning with a painting titled Ganesha as a homage to the traditional Hindu deity of remover of obstacles, Husain went on to paint triptychs titled, Three Dynasties, Language of Stone, Traditional Indian Festivals, Indian Households, Modes of Transport, Tale of Three Cities, Indian Dance Forms and Hindu Triad. Husain was still working on this series when he passed away in London on 9 June 2011.

Legacy

The prolific painter completed an estimated 40,000 paintings during his long dynamic career. M.F. Husain is today credited with taking Indian art out of government patronage to the global marketplace as much as mingling it with popular cultural expressions like films in India. More importantly, he pioneered modernism in India. Heavily influenced by Post-Impressionism, Cubism, Expressionism, he drew upon avant-garde styles to convey Indian themes and subjects. The result was a highly individualistic, vivacious, larger-than-life artistic idiom that would prove to be the precursor of contemporary Indian art wherein Indian painters like V. Gaitonde, S.H. Reza, Tyeb Mehta, Anjali Ela Menon have broken away from traditional techniques and have evolved an eclectic style.

Trivia

- Nicknamed the 'Barefoot Picasso', Hussain was known for never wearing shoes to which he actually credited his phenomenal energy: 'It is good for my knees, it means I can sit on the floor and paint for four or five hours.'
- At one time, Hussain was such a great fan of Bollywood actor Madhuri Dixit that he signed his name on some paintings as 'Madhuri Fida Husain'.
- During his term in the Rajya Sabha, Husain never spoke but simply sat with a sketchbook, drawing his take on the proceedings, which was later published as well.

Conclusion

In August 2018, Christie's—New York's most famous auction portal for fine arts—sold a work titled Portrait of Edmond de Bellomy for US$ 432,000. The subject's face is a golden blur against a dark background and its eyes are black smudges—almost evoking the thick brushstrokes of the Impressionists. But what was so special about it that it made headlines on the Culture pages of the papers that day? The portrait was the first artwork generated by Artificial Intelligence to be sold at Christie's. It had been produced as a result of algorithms by comparing 15,000 pre-twentieth century actual portraits and the whole project was the brain child of a French collective known as Obvious.

So why is this incident significant? Does it mean that art is no longer the sole preserve of human faculties? Or do its implications go further to indicate that AI can also conceptualize its own version of the world? The news made art historians, critics and art lovers of the world rethink the meaning of art and the direction of future artistic conventions. The general consensus was that since all artistic movements through history have constantly sought to innovate, there is some logic for AI to be able to anticipate future conventions and come up with a composition. But is that all art is? Not at all. To create true art, AI would have to make the leap from just an intelligence to an autonomous centre of consciousness that is both rational *and* emotional, that can, not just knock out a combination of lines, shapes and colours, but also *wish* to communicate to viewers its own ideas, perceptions and feelings. This is exactly what the greatest artists down the ages have excelled in. Starting from Renaissance Masters like da Vinci and Michelangelo right down to Pop Art icons like Andy Warhol, the creative minds have been those that take from their past and present surroundings themes, materials and media to fashion their own understanding of the world and beauty so that people can see, discuss and be inspired. Till the time that a robot can do all this and consciously so art remains the product of human intelligence and senses.

Acknowledgements

I wish to thank my editors at Rupa Publications, Saswati, Sourya and Aparna, for ensuring a perfect, publication-ready copy.

I thank my parents for continuing to look forward to the release of my books.

And above all, thank you, dear husband for giving me the space—literally and figuratively—to write.